# 42
# YEARS IN THE
# CLASSROOM

## Lessons I've Learned from Kids, Critters, and Colleagues

**BY JOSEPH RUHL**

With Illustrations by Stacie Takahashi

To my wife, Gail Evans Ruhl—my love, my rock, my example,
and the *heart* of our family.

# ACKNOWLEDGEMENTS

I would like to thank the following people for their love and support, their help and encouragement, and their inspiration:

My wife, Gail, who has loved me unconditionally and always encouraged me. I am so thankful to travel the road of life with her.

My children and grandchildren—our daughter Alison Wade, her husband Will, their daughters Mollyann and Abigail. Our son, Patrick, his wife Jen, and their sons, Dean and Silas. Their faith, love, and joy continually remind me of the blessing of family.

My parents—Dean and Bonnie Ruhl, my first teachers who provided a wonderful childhood for me and my siblings, taught us how to work, and showed us what faith and commitment look like.

My siblings—Dana, Dan, Mark, and Kelly. They were my first friends and fellow budding naturalists as together we explored the forests and streams of our childhood. They and their families continue to be a source of joy and encouragement.

Gail's parents, Howard and Erica Evans, who welcomed me with open arms into their family. I am thankful to be their favorite son-in-law because I'm their *only* son-in-law! I'll always appreciate all those skeletons, skulls, fossils, and preserved specimens that Dad (Dr. Howard Evans, retired professor of Veterinary Anatomy at Cornell University) has given me through the years. Those teaching tools caught the attention of and inspired hundreds of students through the years.

Dr. Sam Postlethwait, botany professor at Purdue University, who instilled in me a love of biology and showed me how much fun teaching could be.

Dr. Jane Butler Kahle, my Purdue biology education professor, who taught me how to teach, and most importantly, encouraged me when I doubted myself.

My teaching colleagues who have mentored me more than they might realize: Steve Randak, Tom Watts, Marge McIlwain, Tom Mertens, Jon Hendrix, Gordon Mendenhall, Sam Rhine, John Wibbens, Charlie Drewes, Ronnee Yashon, Deborah Dillon, David O'Brien, Andrew DeWoody, Amy Lossie, Marshall Overley, Clark Gedney, David Hunt, Clare Lutgen, Amy Heath, Beth Walker, Brian Martin, Debbie and Gregg Beck, Kevin Igo, Bill Huston, and Chuck Herber.

The thousands of students through the years with whom I have been privileged to share the joys of science.

# ABOUT THIS BOOK

Thank you for picking up this book! I feel extremely fortunate to have had the opportunity to teach and coach junior and senior high students for four plus decades of my life. I *hope* my students through the years retained some of the things I tried to teach them, and I *know* that they have taught me important lessons. I have been richly blessed with the friendship of my colleagues in the local schools I taught in, as well as colleagues throughout the state, the nation, and in recent years (through workshops and keynote talks), the world. I love the educators I have known and worked with, and they have inspired me with their intelligence, courage, creativity, entrepreneurial spirit, energy, stamina, compassion, and grit. I love educators because they have a heart for kids. And because they are involved in one of the most important professions on the planet. In this book, you will find me "speaking from the heart," as I share with you the joys, challenges, blood, sweat, tears, heartaches, rewards, and funny (as well as not so funny) stories from my forty-two-year career in the classroom. This book is partly a memoir because within its pages you will encounter some of my reminiscences. It's gratifying for me, and I've been surprised to discover how young teachers have found my "teacher tales" to be helpful as they embark on their own professional journeys. This book is also filled with suggested teaching techniques. My hope is that new and veteran teachers alike will discover a wealth of ready to implement, practical, nontraditional, uncommon, tried and tested tips and tricks within these pages; techniques that I wish I had known when I first started out as a young, novice teacher in the fall of 1978. Among the many lessons shared in this book, I'll describe how transitioning from a teacher-centered classroom to a student-centered classroom freed me up to not only teach, but to coach, mentor, nurture, and inspire my students. I'll share how moving to a student-centered approach enabled me to not only teach my content, but to also engage my students in the six Cs: CHOICE, COLLABORATION, COMMUNICATION, CRITICAL THINKING, CREATIVITY, AND CARING. You will find that many of the ideas shared in chapters 1 through 6 as well as the Conclusion, can be applied to any grade level or content area. Chapters 7 through 10 are specific to teaching biology courses and preparing students for science fair project work. Even if you teach subjects or grade levels other than high school biology, I predict that you will still find some good ideas in the later chapters, especially Chapter 7. Chapter 7 tells the story of a time when non-educators/special interest groups attempted to exert control over our biology curriculum, and I think you will find that story to be interesting. No subject areas are immune to meddling by vocal, influential laypersons; witness for example the recent attempts by outside groups to influence the way that racism is dealt with in U.S. History classes, or the critical public scrutiny that athletic coaches have always had to endure. It's important for educators to be prepared for such challenges.

I haven't always known it, but I've learned in the last 20 or so trips around the sun, that true happiness and fulfillment in life lie not in the accumulation of "stuff," but rather in the cultivation of human relationships. Teaching provides a wonderful opportunity to live out that philosophy. My hope and prayer is that the life-long relationships that you will build with kids, parents, and colleagues will be a blessing to you, as they have been to me!

# INTRODUCTION

I *loved* teaching, but as a retired teacher I must confess that as of this writing, my heart is heavy because I see teachers leaving the profession in droves. Precious few college students are opting to enroll in teacher training programs in colleges and universities throughout the country because more and more unrealistic expectations are being placed upon teachers. I get it. I remember very well what it was like for my colleagues and me as we strove to be the best teachers we could be despite all the other "stuff" that lobbying special interest groups and some state legislators kept piling onto our already overflowing plates. Many times, I had to remind myself to focus on the positives; my love for my students, my passion for teaching, and the thrill of seeing "my kids'" eyes light up when they finally "got it." I had to remind myself to filter out (as much as possible) the negatives such as time-consuming, state-mandated standardized testing and the tedious "administrivia" of filling out required accountability paperwork to document and prove that we were actually doing our jobs in our classes. I know that right now, as a result of what I'll call "societal micromanaging," additional demands of teachers are being considered. Some groups are demanding more parental control over what content will be taught in classes, along with requirements for teachers to submit detailed, publicly scrutinized lesson plans. Other groups are pushing for the removal of books that they deem to be inappropriate from school libraries. There is even talk in some state legislatures of arming teachers to thwart future possible tragic school shootings (*Sigh.*) Despite these challenges, I'm still convinced that the positives—the joys and rewards of this most important and noble of professions—far outweigh the negatives! If you are considering a career in teaching, I know you will find the work to be challenging, but I also know that you can find enjoyment and fulfillment in it. So, I thank you for accompanying me on this retrospective journey as I share with you the joys, challenges, blood (*literally; you'll see!*), sweat, tears, heartaches, and most importantly, the rewards of teaching that I've experienced over my forty-two-year career as a teacher of high school science courses. I retired on June 1, 2020, and I loved teaching "my kids" up until my very last day, so walking away after forty-two years in the classroom was bittersweet. But I thought that forty-two years, which may end up being half of my life, was a pretty good run, and it brought to my mind the words of the Apostle Paul in 2 Timothy 4:7 (*admittedly taken out of context*), "I have fought the good fight, I have finished the race, I have kept the faith."[1] And besides, I felt it was time to retire because our grandchildren who live a four-hour drive away in one direction and a nine-hour drive in the other direction, won't stay little for long!

Why, in this my second year of retirement, have I decided to write this book? There are a couple reasons, one being admittedly selfish, and the other more altruistic. First, even though teaching is hard work (*just ask any teacher!*), when I think back on my years in the classroom, most of those memories are happy, humorous, and richly rewarding, leading me to think that maybe I made a difference in the lives of some of the thousands of students that I worked with. Those memories bring smiles to my face and it is a joy to share those experiences with you. I absolutely *love* sharing teaching ideas—tips and techniques I've learned that I wish I had known when I first started out during the 1978–79 school year. Maybe sharing in this way is such a joy for me because our brains appear to be wired for giving (*Ever experience the "helper's high" triggered by endorphins in the brain when giving to someone else? So maybe this reason is the selfish one.*). It is my hope that young teachers might benefit from what I have learned. Secondly, since I sincerely believe that teaching is one of the most important professions on the planet, I feel a responsibility to share what I've learned with pre-service, beginning, and experienced educators, **and most importantly, to serve as a voice of encouragement**. Surely close to half a century has taught me *something*! (*Maybe that's the altruistic reason.*).

During most of my forty-two years in the classroom, I taught remedial ninth grade general science, ninth grade biology, a junior/senior level elective course in human genetics, and a junior/senior level elective course in science research projects. I always told my friends who were not involved in education that I thought I had the best job in the world because I was able to work with people who were fun, funny, energetic, creative, and insightful, and they happened to be 14 to 18 years of age. I really believe that kids keep a person young at heart!

If you are a teacher of preschool children or kindergarten through eighth grade, please stay with me! Much of the philosophy and many of the strategies that I will share in this book, especially chapters 1 through 6, work with students of all ages, even up through college age. Here's a sneak preview of those first six chapters:

Chapter 1 - **"42 Years in the Classroom? Are You Crazy?"**

In this chapter, I'll describe what kept me going for all those years as a teacher.

Chapter 2 – **The Power of Love in Teaching**

In this chapter, we'll look at teacher caring (*agape* love). It is the most powerful teaching technique known because it enables the teacher to cultivate positive teacher-student relationships that are vital for effective teaching and learning.

Chapter 3 - **How Can We Show Our Students That We Care?**

In this chapter, I'll talk about some practical "nuts and bolts" ways to unleash the power of love in teaching.

Chapter 4 - **Life Lessons I've Learned as a Teacher**

In Chapter 4, I'll share how my students and a large reptile taught me how making myself vulnerable, having compassion, being an encourager, being a risk taker, and learning from humiliating experiences made me a better teacher.

Chapter 5 – **Risky Behavior**

In Chapter 5, I'll share examples of times when I took huge risks by stepping out of my comfort zone to provide my students with uncommon experiences that resulted in improved student motivation and learning.

Chapter 6 - **Transitioning from a Teacher-centered to a Student-centered Classroom**

In Chapter 6, we'll look at how transitioning to a student-centered classroom reignited my passion for teaching and my students' love for learning.

Some of the teaching strategies described in chapters 7 through 10 of this book are specific to biology, human genetics, and science research projects courses, but even if you are a high school teacher in an area other than science, I'm sure you will likely find some ideas that you can apply in your own subject area as well. Here's a quick look at what you will find in chapters 7 through 10:

Chapter 7 – **"May We Live in Interesting Times."**

This chapter tells the story of a stressful time of controversy when I was serving as our school's science department head. It was a time when my fellow biology teachers and I resisted pressure from students and community members to teach creationism alongside evolution in our biology classes. We reluctantly ended up in the national spotlight!

Chapter 8 - **Evolution Teaching Resources**

In Chapter 8, you will find some activities for teaching about evolution in high school biology classes.

Chapter 9 - **More Biology Teaching Resources**

In Chapter 9, I will share more strategies for teaching various biology concepts.

Chapter 10 - **How to Set Up a Science Research Projects Course**

In Chapter 10, I'll describe, step-by-step, how to create and run an independent projects course.

If you're not an educator—and I believe educators include teachers, administrators, guidance counselors, librarians, custodians, technology support persons, school bus drivers, aides, coaches, cafeteria workers, school secretaries, and parents—you're still involved in education, just as the African proverb reminds us, "It takes a village to raise a child." So, come join me on this journey and reignite your love for kids and teaching!!

# CHAPTER 1

# "42 Years in the Classroom? Are You Crazy?"

People have asked me, "Joe, how did you manage to teach kids for forty-two years? What kept you going?" There were several things. First, I believe that for me, teaching wasn't just a job, it was a calling. I LOVED teaching and the opportunities to inspire my students daily, sharing my passion for teaching with them as well as with fellow teachers. I think that's the evidence that it was a calling. Was it hard work? Most definitely, but I found it fulfilling and rewarding. I am convinced that teaching is a noble profession because teachers have the opportunity to leave a small part of the world a little bit better than they found it. The words of the late Christa McAuliffe, teacher and astronaut, have always resonated with me: "I touch the future. I teach."[1] Whenever I walked into the school building on those dark, early mornings, even if I was dead-tired, I knew that what I was doing was important and that I was part of something much bigger than myself. If you are a teacher, please never forget that you are engaged in one of the most important professions on earth. When they're honest, kids know this, even though they may not admit it publicly. Parents know this, and one of the painful lessons the world has learned over the last two years of the COVID-19 pandemic with its school shutdowns and virtual at-home "learning," is just how vital in-person learning with a professional educator is. I've heard adults say, "You're a teacher? I could *never* do that." And then I think to myself "You're probably right because not just *anybody* can do it!" Teaching requires a unique mix of compassion and toughness or grit (*The same is true of nurses—as we've seen during the pandemic.*). Thinking adults know how important teachers are. Not long ago, I was standing in the check-out line at the grocery store and I struck up a conversation with a couple of total strangers behind me and in front of me. The guy behind me as it turned out, was an insurance agent, and the woman in front of me was a receptionist in one of the academic departments at nearby Purdue University. The woman asked me, "And what do you do when you're not standing in line at the grocery store?" When I told them I was a teacher, I sensed in their words and their facial expressions a genuine respect for our work. I would even go so far as to say that I saw in their eyes not just respect for teachers, but a sense of reverence for the work that we do, because most *thinking* people really do have a heart for children. What else kept me going? I'm a biologist, and teaching my subject—biology— allowed me to engage in my passion—that is, to do biology and share that passion for biology and the natural world with my students every day. Teaching biology even provided me with professionally invigorating travel opportunities such as a grant funded trip to the Galapagos Islands located 600 miles west of Ecuador. This experience provided me with inspiration, photos, and videos that enabled me to make my lessons in ecology, botany, zoology, and evolution come alive for my students in a more personal way.

**Figure 1-1** Teaching biology allowed me to *do* biology.

**Figure 1-2** A Teacher Creativity Fellowship grant funded by Lilly Endowment, Inc. enabled me to travel to the Galapagos Islands.

As I've told numerous young teachers who are starting out, teaching will not make you rich financially, but it is one of the few professional careers that will allow you to be creative. Creative activity, for most of human history, has been reserved for the privileged few who had either inherited a fortune so they didn't *have* to work, or who were able somehow, to carve out free time from the daily grind of work and busyness to engage in creating music, art, or literature. Creativity is a uniquely human, pleasurable, satisfying activity. (*I'm sure that our Neanderthal ancestors must have had smiles on their faces when they created those cave paintings!*) I derived a great deal of joy from creating nontraditional learning experiences that would get my students excited about biology. I was the beneficiary of that creative work because I found that when I created a learning activity that was unusual or unexpected (*throw out the old "read the chapter and answer the questions at the end" approach!*), the students really turned on, engaged, and even enjoyed the experience. When I saw the students respond like that, it gave me joy and a rich feeling of satisfaction, and that, in turn, motivated me even more. I found that the more I put into my teaching, the more I got out of it. I always loved the challenge and even made a game of it for myself whenever a ninth grader on the first day of school would express in words or body language, "I've never liked science and I've never been good at it." I remember thinking to myself in those situations, "Okay, kid. Game on! Just wait!"

Sometimes, engaging students in out-of-the-ordinary kinds of learning strategies can create unexpected, positive responses from students that can be a real blessing to the tired spirit of a teacher. I have so many fond memories of those instances of serendipitous joy. One involved what I simply call the pond water lab. It was an activity that I had my ninth grade biology students do early in the school year, within the first week when they were expecting to hear about the usual hundreds of classroom rules, policies, and expectations like they had heard every year in mid-August. Instead, before the students arrived at school, I placed a few buckets of pond water that I had collected the weekend before on one of the lab tables, along with turkey basters, eye droppers, Petri dishes, copies of a guide for identifying pond water macroinvertebrates, and binocular dissecting microscopes on all the other lab tables. When the students arrived, I told them that since this is biology class, we're going to start doing biology! I gave them simple instructions: "Pick a couple partners to work with. Take a turkey baster and suck up some pond water from one of the buckets, squirt it into a Petri dish, take the dish to your dissecting microscope, place the dish under your microscope, and find and draw four different creatures that you have discovered in your Petri dish. Then use the pond water guide to identify each of your four creatures and label each drawing with its common or scientific name." To provide the students with an eye-popping experience, when I collected the buckets of pond water the Saturday before classes, I concentrated the tiny microscopic invertebrates hundreds of times above the population density that one would normally find in a pond water sample, so that the students wouldn't miss the swarms of beautiful, strange, transparent, dancing creatures when they peered through their microscopes. If you're a biology teacher and you want to do this activity, you'll need a pair of waders, a few buckets, and access to a pond or swamp containing undisturbed still water (*the murkier the better!*), preferably with lots of aquatic weeds below the surface and duckweed covering the surface. The most important piece of your equipment will be an easy-to-construct Pour-Person plankton net made of a wooden embroidery hoop with screw tightening mechanism, and a sheet of heavy chiffon fabric or light-weight nylon. I got the idea for this tool from Dr. Charlie Drewes of Iowa State University and you can find the instructions for how to make this plankton net at https://www.eeob.iastate.edu/faculty/DrewesC/htdocs/toolbox-II.htm. As Charlie said, "To use this net in the field, water is collected from a dock or shoreline in a pail-sized container. The net is held by one person while another pours the water sample(s) through the net. The sieved materials (*containing the tiny creatures collectively called plankton*) are then back-flushed into a collection container. Alternatively, the net may be handheld vertically and guided through pond water using figure-eight motions. Then, the concentrated plankton are backflushed into a storage container."[2] The buckets of pond water in the classroom are then so concentrated with the tiny creatures that the students can't miss them! When the students started looking through their microscopes, oh how much fun it was for me to hear their joyous expressions of amazement! Witnessing the thrill of discovery that they were experiencing made this teacher's spirit soar! Oh, the joy of seeing a student grab the arm of their lab partner and enthusiastically exclaim, "Look in here! You've got to see this!" I just stood there and enjoyed the moment (*actually, it was more like forty-five minutes*) as every one of those twenty-five ninth graders was mesmerized for the entire class period. Of course, I didn't just stand there and soak up the satisfaction for the entire period. I wandered around from group to group and responded to their questions: "I've never used a microscope like this. How do you make it focus?" "These little guys in my Petri dish look like little bumper cars. How do they move around?" "What is this creature? I can't find it in the book." Now that's when real learning occurs. Just put the students into a situation where you create in them a need to know and then *they* will begin initiating the questions.

**Figure 1-3** Put the students into situations where you create in them a need to know, and then *they* will begin initiating the questions.

When a girl shouted from the other side of the room, "Mr. Ruhl, come here! You have got to see this! There's something under my microscope that is having babies!" I made a beeline for her lab table and peered through the binocular eyepieces of her microscope. Sure enough! There was a tiny microscopic creature giving birth. The organism was a crustacean known as Daphnia, a diminutive cousin of crayfish, lobsters, and crabs. These Daphnia, never before seen by fourteen- and fifteen-year-olds, are transparent and you can even see their tiny pulsing internal organs. As I gazed into the microscope, I could see tiny, squirming baby Daphnia—exact "mini-me" versions of their mother—visible inside of the mother's body and they were popping out one by one! It was a thrill for me because I had never seen that in my entire life! Suddenly the whole class was lined up behind her microscope waiting for a chance to witness the miracle of life while the girl who made the discovery beamed with pride. I'll never forget how some of the students didn't even want to go to their next class when the bell rang signaling the end of the period, and some even asked if they could come in after school to do this some more! I overheard a student (*not the strongest student academically*) after class in the hallway during passing period when he met up with his friend. The satisfaction that I felt when I heard that student say, "I love biology because we get to do stuff in there!" was a little like the feeling I remembered as a young kid after hitting a homerun in baseball or catching a huge largemouth bass. Many of the rewards in teaching are precious beyond mere dollars and cents. This guided inquiry lesson was designed to do three things. First, to introduce them to the concept of biodiversity, specifically the biodiversity that is literally under their noses. The second purpose was for them to *discover* how to use the microscope. The third and perhaps most important purpose of the activity was simply to whet their appetites and show the students just how cool biology is!

I do admit, it wasn't always fun. My dad was right! When I was growing up, on more than one occasion, Dean Ruhl told me, "Son, sometimes there will be times in life when you have things that just have to be done that you don't want to do, no matter what profession in life you choose." I was the oldest of five children in our family and we had a very large vegetable garden. I vividly remember more than one summer morning when Dad gave that paternal lesson to this seventh grader before he headed off to work. "Joe, I want you to weed the garden before I get home tonight." It seemed like those rows of corn stretched to the horizon! The days of teaching in my adult life that are sort of like weeding the entire garden are those days at the end of the school year when our students in Indiana (*as in other states*) are deprived of valuable instructional time as we dutifully administer a battery of state-mandated standardized tests. The tests have been mandated by state level politicians and bureaucrats, and the students' test scores are used in their teachers' overall yearly evaluations, partly serving as data to be used in calculating teachers' pay raises. These state-mandated standardized tests are based on state-mandated standards that exist for each subject and grade level. I've had biology teachers tell me that the pond water activity at the very beginning of the school year sounds like a neat way to get kids excited about learning biology, but then a few will ask, "But what state standard(s) is the activity connected to?" (*That would be me you hear sighing . . .*). As I've advised so many young teachers who are starting out, "The standards are important, but please don't let them stifle your professional creativity!" When there's a choice between obsessing over whether a class activity is connected to a specific standard versus taking advantage of an opportunity to inspire the students, I will always choose the latter.

# CHAPTER 2

# The Power of Love in Teaching

Now that I've retired, I have found myself with a little more time to reflect and philosophize, and one of the big questions in life that I've thought about is this one: "What's the secret to true happiness and fulfillment in life?" The media, advertisements, and society in general will tell us that the secret to happiness and success is to work hard for most of your life, maybe at a job that you don't really find satisfying, so you can make lots of money and buy lots of stuff (*which you then find yourself spending most of your free time taking care of and fixing your stuff*). Then, when you retire and downsize, you move into a smaller place and get rid of all the stuff you've accumulated. Is that really the American dream? No! I really don't think that's the secret to true happiness and fulfillment. The COVID-19 pandemic of the last couple years, if it has taught us anything at all, has taught us that the secret to true happiness and fulfillment is *relationships*. As I write this, for two years now, covid has deprived us of smiles because of the medically sound and necessary practice of wearing masks. We've been deprived of handshakes and hugs. It has hampered our opportunities to be with loved ones, and not just loved ones at family reunions, weddings, or funerals, but even with strangers—fellow human beings—in restaurants, theaters, concerts, and athletic events. The social distancing and lockdowns have been important safeguards for our health, but they have painfully reminded us of just how much we value relationships. Why, with all the isolation we've experienced, are so many people hurting physically, emotionally, and psychologically? I think the reason is because our brains are wired to be social. Think about our early prehistoric hominid ancestors out hunting for food.

**Figure 2-1** Early humans hunting for food

Those Neanderthals and early *Homo sapiens*, who were good at social behavior, had a better chance of surviving than did the occasional loner. If you were a prehistoric human ancestor, who tried to take on a woolly mammoth or mastodon by yourself, you probably would not have survived and produced offspring that eventually led to us! We are a social species. And not only that, but our brains appear to be wired for loving and being loved. These are good reasons why I think we've missed the smiles, the handshakes, and the hugs. I'm convinced that this has implications for the classroom. After all, life in the classroom is a big part of life. So, what's the secret to true happiness and fulfillment in the classroom? *Relationships!* I'm talking about meaningful, positive relationships between the students, and meaningful, positive, appropriate relationships between the teacher and the students. Relationship is the key to successful, satisfying educational experiences for both the students and the teacher. Why is it that so many substitute teachers have major problems with the kids, especially the subs that are total strangers to the students? The answer I think is obvious. There's no relationship that has been established. Relationship is huge, and it's built upon a foundation of teacher caring, aka *love*. Being a secondary teacher who loves his subject matter, this is something I had to learn from elementary teachers and special education teachers. None of us is a self-made teacher, and as author and motivational speaker Ken Blanchard has said, "*none of us is as smart as all of us.*"[1] I call this teacher caring, the number one "C" because in Chapter 6, I'll introduce the other five "Cs" that I believe are vital to success in teaching. Forty-two years in the classroom have taught me that when the teacher is intentional about showing the students that they genuinely care about the students as individuals, then walls of resistance to learning can crumble, creating positive experiences for the students and the teacher. Nothing motivates students more than their recognition that the teacher genuinely cares about them. When I finally learned this (*and it's not rocket science!*), those days at school when I was intentional about remembering that "I don't teach biology. I teach *kids* biology," were the days when the students seemed to be most cheerful, most attentive, most engaged, and most on task. Needless to say, those were the days when teaching was the most fun, the most rewarding, and the most punctuated with those moments of serendipitous joy throughout the day.

It's important to remember that especially in education, we educators all stand on the shoulders of giants. The importance of loving our students is not my original idea. Remember Mr. Fred Rogers and his PBS television show, *Mr. Rogers' Neighborhood*? He said that good teaching involved addressing the social and emotional needs, and not just the cognitive. He went on to say that if teachers met the social and emotional needs, then the cognitive would follow.[2] He had it figured out a long time ago! I used to watch his television program with my children when they were young, and I was impressed with how he, from the other side of that television screen, would look into the eyes of the child on our side of that screen, and say or sing to the child messages like, "You're special. I like you. There's nobody just like you." And I've noticed that even though Mr. Rogers' show was aimed at predominantly preschoolers, high school students respond as well when the teacher attends to their social and emotional needs. I learned over the years, that if my ninth grade biology students or my eleventh and twelfth grade genetics students felt welcomed (*social need*), and that I genuinely cared for them as individuals (*emotional need*), then those walls of resistance to learning that some kids had, did crumble, allowing lots of cognitive stuff or content to get through. Each teacher has their own unique way of demonstrating caring. For example, when I was in high school back in the early 1970s in Winamac, Indiana, my varsity football coach, Bill Pugh, was tough on us! Oh, how I remember those two weeks of brutal two-a-day practices in the early August heat and humidity! Mr. Pugh reminded us of a bulldog! *But we knew he loved us.* We never heard him swear or cuss. He was like a marine drill sergeant on the football field but we saw the patient, gentle husband, and father that he was off the field. We understood his explanations for how our suffering and conditioning in practices would prepare us for fun and success once the games began, and that most importantly, we would learn self-discipline. He spoke to our hearts and I'll never forget the life lessons that he taught: "Each person on this team is important. We must work together to achieve." "Success requires 20 percent natural ability and 80 percent guts, sweat, determination, and drive." "If you knock an opponent down, then help him up when the play is over." "If you get knocked down, get right up and throw yourself back into the battle." "Watch how you act in life, because younger ones will be watching you." "Nothing of value is accomplished without sacrifice." On the other hand, my senior English teacher, Iona Nale, was a nurturing, gentle, kindly, grandmotherly type, whose style was very different from Mr. Pugh's, yet we knew she loved us. I remember working very hard in her class simply because I didn't want to let her down.

Sometimes when I'm talking to teachers, I notice that initially, some get a little uncomfortable when I talk about the importance of loving their students. So let me explain. I'm not talking about warm, fuzzy, emotional love here. I'm talking about the kind of love that C.S. Lewis wrote about in his book, *The Four Loves*.[3] In this book, he wrote about the fact that the ancient Greeks had four different words that translate into our one English word, *love*. In many ways the language is much more precise than English. For example, one kind of love is called *storge*, or the love of one's family. It can also mean "liking a lot." This would be, for example, the love I have for chocolate or coffee (*essential supplies for many teachers*). C.S. Lewis also discussed another Greek word for love: *philia*, which is the love between friends. A third kind of love that he described was *eros*, or erotic love. For many teenagers, if you mention the English word "love," this is the form that often comes first to their minds! But then he wrote about a fourth Greek word for love: **agape, the highest and noblest form of love. It is selfless love given even to strangers with no expectation of receiving anything in return.** Christian thinkers like C.S. Lewis have described it as self-sacrificial love that is passionately committed to the well-being of the other. In its most extreme form, it can even involve giving one's life for another. A casual review of the history of warfare will reveal not just one but numerous riveting accounts of a soldier throwing himself on a live hand grenade in the heat of battle to save the lives of his buddies. That's hardcore *agape* love. It doesn't always involve warm, fuzzy feelings, although it can. **This highest form of love is not always emotional, but it is always decisional,** making it possible to obey the command, "Love your neighbor as yourself."[4] So, when I talk about the importance of loving our students, *agape* love is the kind of love I'm talking about. I believe that the fact that *agape* love is decisional rather than emotional, can be great news for teachers because let's face it, not all kids are likeable all the time! Any veteran teacher knows that some children can be quite annoying! But if our students can see that we genuinely care about them as individuals, and that we want what is best for them, they will respond. Mr. Rogers was right after all!

# CHAPTER 3

# How Can We Show Our Students That We Care?

Let's get practical. How can we show students that we care? Here are fourteen practices that I have found to be highly effective.

1. **Stand by the door and greet the students as they arrive at your classroom.**

Beginning about the sixth year of my teaching career, I picked up this idea from an educator and motivational speaker by the name of Harry Wong. On the first day of school, I would stand in the hallway outside of my door and greet the students with a smile, a handshake, and a warm "Hi, I'm Mr. Ruhl! Thank you for taking my class! I am so excited to have you in my class!" (*or some similar greeting*). Most of the students expressed genuine appreciation for this gesture and found it to be refreshingly out of the ordinary. A few of the students looked as if they had seen a ghost! Some kids take a while to warm up. If you lean towards the shy end of the personality continuum, this is an activity that you'll have to work at, but I'm sure you will find it to be an effective way to begin establishing those all-important relationships with your students. Relationship is huge and I used this welcoming gesture to start showing the students that I cared, even before the bell rang to begin class!

2. **Be real and smile on the first day of school.**

I'll never forget the first day of my first year of teaching. I was a new teacher at a large inner-city school in Macon, Georgia. Having grown up amidst the cornfields and family-owned farms of rural Indiana, when I graduated from Purdue University in West Lafayette, I decided it was time to fly the nest and go to an "exotic" faraway land. Central High School in Macon, Georgia, an inner-city school of over a thousand students was about as different from my alma mater, Winamac High School in Winamac, Indiana, a rural school of four hundred students, as north is from south. Small town Winamac, Indiana, doesn't have much in the way of cultural and ethnic diversity; it is strikingly homogeneous. So, I confess that I was in a state of culture shock when I stepped into Central High School that first day of school. During that first year of teaching, I grew tremendously as a person and as a teacher, and I am thankful for my colleagues in that school and the students who grew to love me, and I them. As I look back on myself in the first couple of days that year, my classroom management skills and discipline were, shall I say, less than desirable? I had a lot to learn! I don't think I would have survived had it not been for helpful, more experienced colleagues, who took me by the hand and gave me advice early on, as well as a one-on-one basketball challenge that I reluctantly accepted from one of the school's best basketball players during that first week of school (*What was I thinking!*) More about that in Chapter 4. There was one bit of advice from a colleague that I received that first day that was not really too helpful and I was skeptical, but I listened politely. It was lunchtime on that first day, and I sat there, shell-shocked from my first morning as a teacher! A grizzled, old, burned-out veteran teacher sat down beside me at the table in the teachers' lounge and gave me advice: "Don't smile until Thanksgiving!" I was skeptical because it didn't seem natural and I've learned over four decades that that approach just doesn't work. A smile is a universal, disarming expression of acceptance. Don't be afraid to use it.

**Figure 3-1** Don't smile until Thanksgiving? I don't think so!

**3. Learn the students' names as soon as possible and remember and use them inside and outside of the class. Learn something about their interests outside of your class.**

During the summer of 1986, after having taught for eight years, I attended a four-week intensive course in *Human Genetics and Bioethical Decision-making* at Ball State University in Muncie, Indiana. The professors, Drs. Thomas Mertens and Jon Hendrix, were wonderful, dynamic teachers, who equipped and motivated me to start up a Human Genetics course at Jefferson High School in Lafayette, Indiana—the school where I would remain until I retired in the spring of 2020. On the first day of the course, Tom and Jon engaged us—high school biology teachers from across the country—in a beginning of the school year get-acquainted activity that I have since used in my own classes every year. I found that it helped me to learn my students' names quickly, to begin building a spirit of community in the classroom, and to lay the foundation for establishing those all-important positive relationships between the students as well as between the students and me. The design of the activity is actually very simple. Since the students were so used to hearing the teacher talk about classroom rules and policies on the first day of school, they found this activity a welcome and unexpected break in the routine. I decided to wait until the second day of school to go over classroom rules of which I only had one: "Treat others as you would have them treat you." I did, of course, elaborate a little bit on specific examples of how someone might mess up and not put that rule into practice. But on the first day, to introduce the get-acquainted activity, I always told the students, "Welcome! Thank you for taking my class (*I loved the puzzled looks during this moment.*) I love biology and I can't wait to share it with you, but more importantly, you are more than names and student ID numbers on this printout, so I first want to find out who you are as people. Then we'll get into biology." After that brief introduction, I would then pull up the slide screen to reveal the following list that I had previously printed on the board:

1. Name

2. Birthdate

3. Extracurricular activities

4. Hobbies

5. Part-time job, if any

6. Favorite food

7. Favorite movie

8. What do you want to be when you "grow up?"

After that, I would tell the students to take out a sheet of paper and then to find a partner to talk to (*"What? We can talk in here?"*). Then I would say "Take a few minutes to interview your partner, and to write down the above listed eight pieces of information about your partner on your paper. After you're finished, your partner will interview you, and write down information about you on their paper. When everyone is finished with their interviews, then I'll have you come up to the front of the classroom, one pair at a time, and introduce your partner to the rest of the class." The wide-eyed looks on the faces of some of the students at this time revealed varying levels of anxiety as many teenagers are self-conscious about speaking in front of an audience. I reassured the students and told them that such feelings are normal; everybody has them. I always went on to say something like, "In almost every career or profession that you choose, there will be times when you will have opportunities to speak publicly, so this is a good time to begin practicing!" (*And why not let them share a little bit of the first day of school jitters that this introvert leaning teacher experiences!*) The important unspoken message to the students on this first day of school was that they could expect this class to be student-centered rather than teacher-centered (*more on that in Chapter 6*). The productive buzz that ensued during the next ten minutes while the students interviewed one another was the kind of low-level classroom noise that teachers love to hear—the sound of students working together with purpose. This activity worked especially well for me because many of the students really did not know each other, since our school, where I spent the last thirty-six years of my forty-two-year career (*Jefferson High School in Lafayette, Indiana*) is an urban high school of around two thousand five hundred students in the upper four grades. After all the interviews were completed, I made my way back to the front of the room and brought the class back together with an announcement that went like this: "Before we start the introductions, I think that if I'm having you guys do this, it's only fair that I should go first, so I'll introduce myself!" Now I'm sure that some (*especially ninth graders*) students have the idea that their teacher really doesn't have a life outside of school. I remember thinking that when I was a kid. I remember riding my bicycle out on a country road the summer before my ninth grade when I came upon one of our favorite childhood playgrounds—Indian Creek just before it empties into the Tippecanoe River in Pulaski County, Indiana. There was one of my teachers and junior varsity football coach, Roger Haniford, and he was fishing! And he was wearing blue jeans and a T-shirt! What? He was a real person! Introducing myself to the students as I shared the eight pieces of information about me revealed to the students that I was real and most importantly, approachable.

Before the students began introducing their partners to the rest of the class, I handed out a blank seating chart and told the students to note where they were in the classroom seating arrangement and to print their names on the seating chart (*"You mean we can choose where we want to sit in this class?"*). I also told the students that when all the introductions were completed, I would collect their papers and study them carefully so that I could learn all about who they were as persons. As I sat on a student desk or lab table to the side of the class during the student introductions, I took careful notes on each student, noting especially the correct pronunciations of any unusual names. Having the students pronounce their partners' names during the introductions saved me *and* the students the embarrassment of butchering their names. That's not something that should be done to a self-conscious or insecure student on the first day of school. After each pair presented their partner to the class, I was able to interject occasional remarks such as "You're on the softball team? What position do you play? First base? That's what I played on the baseball team when I was in high school back in the Pleistocene, when woolly mammoths roamed the frozen tundra!" Or "You're going to try out for the school musicals? I can't wait to see you on the stage!"

This first day of school activity took pretty much the entire class period and I would spend some time during the first couple evenings of that first week, studying the students' papers so that when I would see them in the school hallways, I could address them by name and ask them questions such as, "How's your after-school marching band practice going? I've seen you guys out there after school, marching under the hot August sun in the school parking lot!" Or "Has that restaurant that you work at given you a raise yet? No? Does Mr. Ruhl need to go in and talk to your boss?" As you can see, from the beginning, I was trying to be intentional about establishing those all-important appropriate, firm, friendly, and fair teacher-student relationships. Relationship in the classroom is huge.

I've mentioned before that every effective teacher stands on the shoulders of giants (*mentors*). I'll never forget one of those giants. His name was Dr. Sam Postlethwait, the creative innovative pioneer in science education at Purdue University—the father of the student-centered audio-tutorial method of instruction that he used in his freshman biology course, Botany 108. It was early in the fall semester of my freshman year of college. He saw me in the hallway and said, "Hello Joe! How are you?" I was floored and I felt valued! It was only the first week of school, he oversaw a course of hundreds of students, and he knew my name! That was probably the best lesson that I learned on my path towards becoming a teacher.

**Figure 3-2** Dr. Sam Postlethwait—Purdue University Botany professor (and my mentor) and pioneer in science education

### 4. Have a sense of humor. Be able to laugh at yourself.

It's important to find out and be aware of your own unique style of humor. My humor tends to be a bit daffy, of the self-deprecating kind. This style of humor can show the students that their teacher is human, soften their hearts, and help to create a sense of community. For example, I came to school one day with a hard-to-miss, large coffee stain on my light-colored shirt. Ah yes, the hazards of driving with a coffee cup in hand with stop-and-go traffic on the way to school. Sure enough, some kid in first period pointed it out and I responded, "*What* spot? I don't see a spot! Oh that! Oh, *that* must be why they taught us in driver's ed class to keep both hands on the wheel!" I'm not a great joke teller, because my attempts at jokes tend to be "Dad jokes" so I will avoid telling jokes. It's just not my style. Be sure to find out what your style is and use it. Kids respond to humor.

5. **Look prepared and be prepared. Establish regular routines.**

Being prepared is just basic professionalism. Think about how you feel when you dine at a fine restaurant. A professionally dressed host or hostess smiles, welcomes you, and escorts you to your table. You sit down to a beautifully prepared table, complete with pressed white tablecloth, flowers, neatly folded cloth napkins, and carefully placed silverware. The presentation of the food, when it arrives, is so immaculate, you may be tempted to take a photograph of your plate and post it on Instagram! You're made to feel like you're the only customer there, and you just know that this restaurant carefully prepared before opening their doors. Contrast that to the way you felt if you've ever pulled up to the speaker in a fast-food drive-through lane and heard the employee announce, "Our chocolate shake machine is out of order." It probably says a lot about me, but for me that can be a real letdown, especially on a long road trip. Looking prepared and being prepared is just as important in education. Many schools, like my school, had a "teacher prep day" the day before the first day of school for students. There is no way to adequately prepare your classroom on that first 'teacher day' because it will inevitably be filled with meetings. I used to go to work in my classroom a few hours a day a couple weeks before the school year started, just to get things ready. I've always believed that the more you put into your teaching, the more you'll get out of it. Since I taught biology, I always enjoyed turning my classroom into a menagerie to wow the students and grab their attention when they arrived. During those two preparation weeks, I would clean and restock aquariums and animal cages, hang potted plants from the ceiling, hang up eye-catching posters, and make sure my handouts were printed and ready to go. When the students arrived, they were like six-year-olds, who had just entered a toy store. There was a six-foot-long boa constrictor named Bubba, a green iguana named Iggy, a box turtle, painted turtles, fresh water and salt water aquaria, Australian zebra finches, crayfish that I had caught in a local creek a few days before, three-inch-long Madagascar hissing cockroaches, gerbils, and a rabbit named Bun. A huge three-hundred-gallon aquarium with bass and schooling blue gills elicited cries of "Cool!" when the students entered the room.

**Figure 3-3** The bass and schooling bluegills were a hit!

If you're a biology teacher, such a menagerie cannot be easily built in your first year of teaching. It takes time, little by little, to collect the cages and aquaria. It's easier if you find yourself in a school with plenty of financial resources, but if not, get in the habit of stopping at garage sales, where you can find such items at almost giveaway prices. Many of the larger, exotic animals were given to me by people in the community, who didn't want to care for them anymore. The care of the animals and plants through the school year was, I admit, quite a bit of work, so I designated ninth grade biology students—the ones who volunteered—to be responsible for plant and animal care. A couple students became snake experts. A couple took care of the rabbit. A couple were placed in charge of watering the plants, and so on. This relieved me of the responsibility; the students enjoyed it, and they took ownership in not just my classroom, but *our* classroom. Anybody who has been in the classroom knows that some kids just don't seem to have a filter, but sometimes the things they say can warm and delight a teacher's heart. One example is forever imprinted in my memory. I learned that Frank had failed biology the year before, so he was one of a few sophomores taking the class with mostly freshmen. Frank wore the same clothes just about every day. His personal hygiene and home life were sad. His guidance counselor told me that Frank was "at risk" and that he looked forward to quitting school when his sixteenth birthday arrived. As it turns out, Frank blossomed and was a real pro when it came to taking care of the animals, especially the reptiles. The students even learned to respect his knowledge and help. He even knew more about reptile care than I did, as my bachelor's and master's degree work in biology focused mainly on the cellular and molecular aspects of the natural world. I had Frank in first period class and he told me, unfiltered one day, "You know Mr. Ruhl, last year I had tons of tardies, but I ain't had a single tardy this year because I don't want to be late and I love coming in and taking care of the snake and stuff." Now, his grades in biology weren't exactly stellar, but he did pass, and two years later, he graduated from high school.

Now for the second part of this list of practices—establish regular routines. For example, the students knew that they were responsible for their animal/plant care 'chores' during the first ten minutes of the period on Fridays, and those were the only times when they were not required to be in their seats when the tardy bell rang. They knew to head right for their assigned responsibilities as soon as they entered the room. The students knew where the homework box was for handing in papers, they knew where and how to check and monitor their own progress, and they knew where the lab materials were stored and the procedures for obtaining them. I'll go into detail on my efforts to establish regular routines in Chapter 6, but for now, it's important to point out that human beings feel most secure and are most productive when they feel they have "learned the ropes" in their working environment. I know that when I attend a conference in a city and conference center that I'm not familiar with, I feel most secure and most productive after I've spent a little time walking around and becoming familiar with the place; the locations of the coffee shop, restaurant(s), restrooms, meeting rooms, and where my presentation room will be. Even the most adventurous of our species likes to know how to get around.

### 6. Be passionate and excited about what you're teaching.

Margaret McFarland was a child psychologist who happened to be Mr. Fred Rogers' mentor. Here's a quote from her: "Attitudes aren't taught, they're caught. If a teacher has an attitude of enthusiasm for the subject, the student catches that whether the student is in second grade or is in graduate school."[1] I know we've all experienced this. When I was an undergrad student at Purdue University in the early 1970s, I took a course in statistics that (*sorry math teachers!*) was not a course I would have chosen to take if it had not been for my academic advisor and my chosen degree requirements. I struggled with the subject matter and I would rather have been in another biology course or out in a stream or forest collecting specimens. However, the professor in that course sparked my interest and made the class palatable for me, because she was so passionate and excited about statistics. In addition, she used real world, practical examples flavored with pop culture references to illustrate the concepts that she was teaching. It certainly made a difference to this student who, shall I say, *tolerated* math!

I'll never forget my third grade teacher, Miss Hershey. It was 1963 and I attended a tiny, country school surrounded by cornfields, in Milan Center township, Indiana. Tiny Milan Center, in Allen County, Indiana, consisted of not much more than our elementary school building and a grain elevator across the road. Since I had not been back there in 57 years,

I stopped on a drive home from Ohio a couple summers ago just to look around and to reminisce. The apple trees we used to climb in the playground out back (*against the rules!*) were gone. The children, half of whom were Amish, were not to be seen. The old brick school was not in use as a school anymore and it was locked up. With a catch in my throat (*I admit that I'm a bit sentimental*) I tested the front doorknob in vain. I longed to walk on those old polished wood floors again!

**Figure 3-4** The old brick school in Milan Center township, Indiana was not in use as a school anymore and it was locked up.

It felt like a ghost town—not a soul in sight. The quiet of that reflective moment was broken by the charming clip-clop of a horse's hooves as an Amish buggy traveled down the blacktop country road that ran past the front of the building. Again, my mind went back to Miss Hershey. I remember she never yelled, not once. I remember how she picked me to play the role of the prince in our class production of *Cinderella*, and how she allowed me to turn down the starring role and opt for a minor role because I would have to hold Cinderella's hand as we stepped into the chariot. Susie was cute and I secretly liked her, but the thought *(that I, of course, kept to myself)* of sitting next to her in the chariot, scared me to death. (*Five years later, I would have jumped at the chance!*) My most vivid memories of Miss Hershey were the times when she would take 10–15 minutes after lunch to read to us. There she stood at the front of the class each day in her flowered dress, reading a small portion of *The Adventures of Tom Sawyer*, to be continued the next day! Now we had entertaining cartoons on our black-and-white TV at home, but this was different! Reading about the adventures of *Tom Sawyer* was riveting! And at the end of each day's reading, I couldn't wait for Miss Hershey to continue the story the next day. It seemed that Tom and his friends were always at a cliff-hanger when she closed the book for the day! It was obvious to us that Miss Hershey was passionate about reading and loved to read to us! Looking back, I would have to say that she inspired *me* to be a reader. But Miss Hershey taught in a time before non-educators in state legislatures began mandating state-wide standards and standardized testing, so she, being respected by society for her experience and professional training, was free to teach and inspire. I should have looked her up and written her a thank you-letter a long time ago.

I think we can all agree on the importance of the teacher being passionate and excited about what she is teaching. But what about those days when you're just not feeling it? We've all been there. Maybe you've been up most of the night with a sick toddler. Maybe you were up late the night before grading papers or listening to a teenager, who chose 11:30 p.m. as the time when she really wanted to talk. Or maybe you were feeling a cold coming on. Or maybe, as an older, veteran teacher, you were caring for and concerned about aging parents who have taken a downward turn. Or maybe you were thinking about that phone call that you needed to make to the doctor's office later in the afternoon to check on the results of medical tests that you or a loved one has had. Or your furnace has gone out. I'm sure we could all generate a long list here. So, what about those days when you just don't feel like "bringing it?" I stumbled upon the answer long ago, early in my career— *"fake it until you make it!"* I noticed on those days when I just didn't feel it, that if I acted enthusiastic and excited about what I was teaching, it rubbed off on the kids and they engaged positively in the lesson—which in turn ramped up my enjoyment and motivation, which then engaged the kids even more, resulting in passion and enthusiasm in me that was not faked, but authentic. What a lovely example of a positive feedback loop! Years later, I heard one of the best professional development speakers I have ever known. His name is Dave Burgess and he's the author of an outstanding, practical book (*which I highly recommend*) entitled *Teach Like a Pirate*. In this book, he addresses this very topic of teacher passion and enthusiasm, and thanks to Dave, I now know why "fake it until you make it" works. In that memorable professional development meeting, Dave said that this works because "physiology works fast." He writes, "Even if you are only acting at first, an amazing thing happens along the way. You actually start to really feel and become enthusiastic because of your breath pattern and the way you are holding and moving your body."[2] I remember thinking as Dave was speaking, "So that's why acting works!" Sometimes in professional development meetings, we teachers learn something new and sometimes we're simply affirmed (*and do teachers ever need encouragement!*) when we hear that a technique that we've always used is regarded by the experts as being a best practice. Hearing Dave talk about passion and enthusiasm was one of those times when I felt affirmed and thus encouraged.

7. **Allow time for freedom of movement in the classroom along with small group, hands-on work requiring students to *collaborate* and *communicate*.**

For the first few years of my teaching career, my "go to," comfortable, teaching method was lecturing. After all, that was the predominant method of instruction that I grew up with. I think most of us remember the "teacher-centered" classroom. Right? The teacher was up front and center. The students were in nice neat rows, not allowed to talk to each other and the teacher, the source of authority, downloaded information to the kids, who regurgitated it back up on a test designed to measure how much content they could remember. The first few years of my career, I was tempted to resort to that comfortable, familiar style, even if it wasn't exactly inspiring for the students or for me!

**Figure 3-5** I think most of us remember the teacher-centered classroom.

I've already mentioned that we stand on the shoulders of giants. We all have those mentors, whom we are indebted to. Dr. Sam Postlethwait, the Purdue University biology professor I referred to earlier was the first to open my eyes to the world of student-centered teaching. His freshman botany course was individualized in the sense that it was self-paced. There were no lectures! Instead, it was up to me to schedule the time during the week when I would go into the learning center (*it wasn't referred to as the classroom*), where there were twenty or so booths arranged around the perimeter of the large room. I would pick up a printed study guide—a note taking guide—for the week's mini-unit, and then sit down in one of the booths. Each booth was equipped with a tape recorder that contained a cassette tape (*remember, it was 1973!*) of the "lecture." Wearing headphones that were plugged into the tape recorder, I could go at my own pace, rewind, and listen to a segment again if I needed to, or stop the tape and ask for help from one of the teaching assistants (*TAs*)—a few upperclassmen or graduate students in light blue lab coats wandering around the room. I could tell that these TAs were not only biology majors, but people who had been carefully picked by Dr. Postlethwait for their knowledge, nurturing personalities, and passion for teaching. At certain times during the taped lecture, the speaker on the tape (*usually Dr. Postlethwait*) would instruct me to stop the tape and walk to one of the demonstration tables located in the center of the room, where I would engage with one, two, or three other students in a cooperative, hands-on learning experience; for example, examining some aspect of plant anatomy that had been discussed on the tape, or peering through a microscope. Upon completion of the taped mini-unit, I could then sign up for a time slot later that week to take the quiz on that study guide. The quizzes were oral examinations, where I would sit at a round table with a TA and four other students, who had signed up for the same time slot. Keeping score on a notepad, the TA would go around the table asking us questions to test our knowledge of the material. After several rounds of answering questions, the TA would discreetly slip each of us a note with our score on it. I knew that if I didn't pass the quiz, I could retake it later that week. If I passed the quiz, then I knew that my grade for that week's mini-unit was a 'C.' In order to earn points towards a 'B' or an 'A' for the week's mini-unit, I would take a written A/B test at the end of the week. I loved that course! The flexibility and the nontraditional nature of the course were refreshing. I could go at my own pace (*within the limits of a week, of course*) and it forced me to take charge of my own learning, to set goals, and to monitor my own progress. It was individualized because I could go at my own pace (*within certain parameters*) yet it was set in a learning environment that featured small group work, collaboration, and communication with my classmates as well as the

TAs. These innovations in education were revolutionary in the late 1960s and early 1970s.

I did my student-teaching during the spring semester of my senior year of college. In the fall semester of that year, I took a course entitled "Biology Teaching Methods" from a professor by the name of Dr. Jane Butler Kahle. Dr. Kahle had extensive experience herself as a former high school biology teacher. She taught us to "throw out the traditional textbook and lecture approach" and to be innovative and nontraditional. She built on the lessons taught by Sam Postlethwait of the importance of engaging in cooperative learning settings. When I reminisce on my teaching abilities during my first few years as a newbie teacher, honestly, I'm a bit embarrassed. Many of the lessons I taught flopped! In fact, many lessons failed even in the later years of my forty-two-year career! Sometimes a carefully designed lesson just fails to resonate with students. The important thing is to use our failures as learning experiences so that we can grow. Dr. Kahle taught me that. She was a nurturer and an encourager. The message that she conveyed to me was "Joe, you're a new teacher, you're young, but you're a *good* teacher!" As I was an underconfident, somewhat shy and slightly above average student, that encouragement motivated me profoundly! I began to really *believe* that I could teach. Her words motivated me to work hard and to be intentional about striving each year to be a better teacher than I was the year before. Most importantly, I learned from her just how important it is to encourage students—to point out to them and praise them for the things they do well.

**Figure 3-6** Dr. Jane Butler Kahle

For my student teaching experience, Dr. Kahle placed me in a small rural town in northern Indiana known as North Judson. I know I must have been like a "deer in headlights" when I entered North Judson-San Pierre High School that cold wintery day in March of 1977. I was scared to death, wondering if I was up to the task! When I walked into the classroom I was blown away! It was two adjoining classrooms with a large doorway connecting the two. Each of the two rooms was decked out with hanging plants, cages of fascinating animals, and fresh and salt water aquaria with the entire menagerie maintained by active, engaged ninth graders. I had not one supervising biology teacher but two—Tom Watts and Steve Randak—who teamed up to teach, and moved freely between the two rooms. They had been mentored by Dr. Sam Postlethwait and so, one of the rooms was equipped with booths, tape recorders, headphones, study guides, and a round table for the oral quizzes—just like Sam's course at Purdue! The adjacent room was set up for the hands-on lab work. Tom and Steve would alternate days staffing the two different rooms. When I arrived, I became a third member of the team, so on some days, I found myself giving oral quizzes in one room and some days, helping students with their lab work in the other room. Tom Watts and Steve Randak are two of the most innovative high school, biology teachers I have ever known, and I am grateful to them for reinforcing what I had learned from Sam and Jane— the importance of engaging students in hands-on, minds-on, collaborative work. Twenty years later, when I was the science department head at Jefferson High School in Lafayette, Indiana, we hired Steve Randak to join our science department composed of sixteen science teachers. It didn't take long for Steve and me to convince our very supportive, innovation-minded administrators (*thanks to our principal Dennis Blind*) to allow us to install a large door between our two adjacent biology classrooms, and to develop a program similar to what Steve and Tom had run when I taught with them. We brought on board a couple of other outstanding and inspiring biology teachers, Clare McKinney and Amy Heath. The most striking change that a visitor to our classroom would notice was that the tape recorders with the taped "lectures" had been replaced by desktop computers with attached headphones. Steve Randak and I pursued a new hobby—producing computer tutorial lessons that students would work through as they filled out their study guides. We produced teacher-developed computer programs using an authoring program called Adobe Director and we are indebted to another innovative giant, whose shoulders we stand on, Dr. Clark Gedney of the Purdue University Biology Department, who taught Steve and me how to create the programs. After Steve retired, and Clare and Amy moved on to other schools, I continued in my own classroom to run a similar program, modified of course, since I was the only teacher in the room, and I'll share more of that story in Chapter 6.

All of these experiences have taught me the importance of allowing time for students to engage in small group, cooperative, collaborative, hands-on work. Most students enjoy this format and appreciate teachers, who care enough to make the effort to incorporate this learning style into their curriculum. It makes sense that they would like it, because remember, we are a social species. Our brains are wired to collaborate and communicate. I'm convinced that having students sit in nice neat rows, where they're not allowed to talk to each other, is unnatural and counterproductive. Just as important as my own observations of students through the years, the educational research of William Glasser supports this practice. According to Glasser, students learn 10 percent of what they read, 20 percent of what they hear, 30 percent of what they see, 50 percent of what they see and hear, 70 percent of what they discuss with others, 80 percent of what they experience personally, and 95 percent of what they teach others.[3] As I moved about the classroom, it was exciting for me to hear students in their groups working together, exploring, hypothesizing, problem solving, and teaching one another. In short, these activities provided opportunities for students to probe the upper levels of Bloom's taxonomy (*Remember Bloom's Taxonomy from your college teaching methods courses?*) as they engaged in higher-level thinking. A few years ago, some teachers, who visited and observed, were amazed that "100 percent of the kids were on task 100 percent of the time in three consecutive ninety-two-minute periods." For me, teaching this way is not only effective, but it's also fun. It allows the teacher opportunities to informally sit down with small groups of students and respond to questions that *they* initiate.

8. **Allow time for project work. Humans (even teenagers!) enjoy being *creative*.**

I've learned so much from teacher colleagues in other grade levels and subject areas.

I've said, "None of us is as smart as all of us!" (Ken Blanchard) I've noticed that giving students opportunities to engage in project work is something that elementary and middle school teachers, as well as art, music, family/consumer sciences, and vocational education teachers have always been good at. In those subject areas that have traditionally emphasized downloading content into the students' brains (*like my own area—science*), it takes a bit of courage and trust for the teacher to move off-stage and allow the students time for project work. Creativity is a uniquely human, pleasurable, self-satisfying activity. Since human brains are wired for creativity, students like to be given the opportunity for project work, and they view it as evidence that the teacher cares. Just as important, project work is pedagogically sound because it promotes problem-solving and critical thinking. Project work will involve students not just in basic memorization or understanding thinking, but will move them up into those higher levels of thinking such as applying, analyzing, evaluating, and ultimately to the pinnacle of higher-order thinking: creating.

In each unit of my ninth grade biology course, I gave students the opportunity to do a project (*created mostly outside of class time*) if they wanted to earn additional points towards a higher grade for that unit (*more on that in Chapter 6*). I allowed them to design a project of their own choosing that would demonstrate in a nontraditional way their understanding of some concept or topic that they had learned about during the unit. One specific example was quite memorable. It was during the first three-week unit of the school year on the nature of science. I'll never forget a group of four girls who decided to write a script for a fifteen-minute play about the conflict and subsequent trials that Galileo suffered at the hands of church leaders in the 1600s. They then acted out and made a video dramatization of Galileo's discoveries, trial, and sentencing, complete with fake beards and makeshift attempts at period clothing! We watched their entertaining and educational production in class. I really believe that those four girls and their classmates will always remember key aspects of the nature of science taught by Galileo because of this project work. But beyond mere belief, I recall some empirical evidence that project work is effective. A couple of years ago at a high school football game I met Tenecia, a former student who is now a twenty-year veteran of our town's police force. She hugged me and said, "Mr. Ruhl! I'll never forget that cell cake I made for your biology class! I still remember that the mitochondrion is the power house of the cell, that the endoplasmic reticulum moves materials throughout the cell, that the nucleus contains the DNA and controls the cell's activities, and that the vacuoles are storage bins in the cell, (*she went on and on, much to my delight!*) . . ." I remember! She had baked a cake at home and decorated it with icing and different sizes and shapes of various candies to represent the different cell parts, creating a 3D edible model of a cell. When she brought it to school, she gave a five-minute presentation to the class, pointing out the various cell parts and describing their functions. Even though she and her co-workers over the years have likely not talked much in their daily conversations about the importance of mitochondria, the endoplasmic reticulum, the cell nucleus, or vacuoles, she retained that information for all these years, thanks to project work!

9. **Whenever possible, allow for student *choice* of learning activities.**

Autonomy is a universal human value. Humans seem to like it when they know they have choices. Have you ever noticed people moving through the line in a smorgasbord restaurant, picking and choosing the food items to place on their plates? They usually have smiles on their faces because of the opportunity to make choices! I have seen my own toddler-aged grandchildren behave much more positively when their very wise, kindergarten teacher mother has given them choices: "You may have a cookie after dinner, but first, you must either take one more bite of your green beans or one more bite of your salad." "Your younger brother loves to play with your toys too. So, you get to pick which toy to let him play with for a while—either your truck or your basketball." In all aspects of life, humans like having choices, and that includes life in the classroom. The following are a few easy-to-implement, simple ideas that can be used to allow for student choice in many different grade levels and subject areas. I am certain you have used some of these and that you have other ideas as well. I believe it's important for us to be reminded to implement student choice whenever we can.

1. Allow choices on tests or quizzes. When I was a college student, I took a course in Cell Biology and the professor would often give us essay tests with the following instruction: "Do any three of the following five essay questions."

2. Choose which homework problems to do. When I was a high school student, I remember a math teacher who told us, "For homework, do either the odd or the even-numbered problems at the end of the chapter."

3. "Design and construct a project of your own choosing that would demonstrate in a nontraditional way, your understanding of some concept or topic that you learned about during the unit." (*Sound familiar?*)

4. "Here are three activities that I have set up at three different learning stations throughout the classroom. When you have completed the work at the three stations, go ahead and hand in your work. You may rotate through the stations in any order you choose."

5. "Here are some practice genetics problems I would like for you to work on. You may either work alone or with a partner."

6. (*On the first day of school*) "You may sit anywhere you want (*I'll check in a week or two to see if it works out!*), and I'll pass around a blank seating chart for you to print your name on."

7. "For today's group work, you may choose your lab partners."

Kids like a class in which they have choices. If you give them choices, they will believe and *know* that you care. I'm looking forward to Chapter 6, where I will describe in detail, how I converted my ninth grade biology course to a one-teacher-in-the-room (*without TAs or a team teacher*), student-centered classroom based almost completely on student-choice.

## 10. Recognize students for their accomplishments outside of the classroom.

Human beings have a desire to be successful in whatever passion in life they choose to pursue, and to feel a sense of pride in a job well done. I also believe human beings have an inherent need to feel valued and to be recognized. I have found recognizing students for their accomplishments outside of the classroom to be a powerfully effective way to show the kids that I care, and to strengthen those all-important teacher-student relationships in the classroom. To do this, whenever I had a student recognized in the local newspaper for some accomplishment in an outside activity such as Chess Club, the school play or musical, choir, Robotics Team, 4-H fair queen, Eagle Scout award, or athletics, I always enjoyed cutting out their newspaper article and posting it on the Wall of Fame in my classroom. It was a simple thing to do but so effective! Even if a student never made the newspaper, the unspoken message when they saw the Wall of Fame covered with newspaper articles, was that this teacher cared. I always loved it when a student would make eye contact with me and smile when they recognized their news clipping on the wall. I would normally say something like, "I was so excited to see that in the newspaper this morning! How cool! I'm proud of you! Please take a pen and, sometime this period, sign that newspaper article, because someday when you're famous, I bet your autograph will be worth lots of money and it will help fund my retirement!"

**Figure 3-7** Our classroom Wall of Fame

There is one student who I know I'll never forget. She walked into my ninth grade biology class on the first day of school with a perpetual frown, a "chip on her shoulder," and body language that shouted out that she and I were not going to get along this school year. Classroom teaching experience taught me to not take a student's negative attitudes or behaviors personally. (*It's not always easy to remember this!*) Who knows what might be happening in the student's home life or in the hours leading up to class? Besides, mood changes are often just a normal part of the adolescent body and mind. But in her case, this continued every single day. As a result, her negative attitude affected her productivity in class and her grades were dismal. This went on until later in the fall when basketball practices started up and the games began. As it turned out, even though she was only a freshman, she was the girls' varsity team point guard, team leader, and leading scorer! It wasn't long before she was featured in the sports section of the newspaper. When the first article came out featuring an action-photo of an exciting three-point shot that she made at the buzzer to beat a rival team, I cut it out and taped it on the wall early in the morning, long before the students arrived. When she arrived and sat down in class that day, I watched her. She slowly and discreetly turned her head towards the Wall of Fame. She certainly did not want me or anyone else to see her glance up there! And then she saw it. That was the first time I saw her smile! She made eye contact with me and oh, that smile! I told her, "You're a ninth grader and the leading scorer on your team! I am so proud of you and I can't wait to see you play in person! When is your next game?" From that day on, she took ownership of her work in the class, and her productivity increased resulting in grades that steadily improved as the semester progressed. Was that simple gesture on my part the thing that turned her around in that class? I've learned to try to maintain a spirit of humility in such cases. Sometimes it can be difficult to accurately link a specific effect or outcome back to its actual cause. Maybe a friend, guidance counselor, basketball coach, or parent motivated her to "get on the stick." Who knows? What I do know, is that our relationship in the classroom changed dramatically. From that day forward, whenever she saw me in the hallway or in the lunchroom, she would greet me with a smile and a "Hi Mr. Ruhl! How are you this morning?" She began doing 'A' work! Sometime closer to the end of that semester, an English teacher pulled me aside in the teachers' lounge and said, "Joe, I need to tell you, Lorraine (*I'm not using the student's actual name*) told me that Mr. Ruhl's biology class is her favorite class!" As I think about this student now and then, what a precious memory. But if you're reading this, please hear me. Over the course of my years in the classroom, was I able to "save" them all? If you're an experienced teacher I'm sure you know the answer to that one. Of course, I had my share of failures as well as successes in teaching. But hey, compare our profession to that of, for example, a major league baseball player. If a professional baseball player gets a hit three out of every ten trips to the plate (*a .300 batting average*), and maintains that 30 percent success rate throughout his entire career, he'll end up in the Hall of Fame! Hopefully, as educators, we'll do better than 30 percent! I couldn't win over each and every kid, just like, as I've mentioned before, there were days when I designed and delivered a lesson that would flop. But that's the way life is in any profession. You do your best. You pick yourself up, dust yourself off, reflect on what went wrong with that lesson, and think about how you would teach it differently the next time. Every summer for forty-two years, I took a little time to rewrite lessons that didn't go as well as I would have liked for them to have gone. My goal each year was to strive to be a better teacher than I was the year before.

My wife and I sometimes like to vacation on Sanibel Island in Florida. Whenever I run across a live starfish on the beach, the child in me reaches down to pick it up (*that bending over motion actually gets a little more difficult with each passing year!*). The biologist in me is thrilled at examining the intricate system of undulating tube feet on its ventral side, and then the teacher in me is tempted to gently toss it back into the rolling surf. Why? In moments like that, my thoughts return to teaching, and a story that you may be familiar with, originally penned by Loren Eisley called *The Starfish Story*. If you've not heard of it, it's a beautiful parable about public service in general, and specifically, about our desires as teachers to reach each student.[4] It goes something like this. A gentleman was strolling on the beach one day and he came upon a little boy who was picking up starfish and throwing them back into the ocean. He asked the child why he was doing that and the child responded, "I have to throw them back into the water or else they'll die." The man smugly replied, "Son, there are hundreds of starfish scattered on miles of beaches. You're not going to make a difference." The polite little boy picked up another stranded starfish, smiled, tossed it back into the surf, and said, "I made a difference for that one."

**Figure 3-8** The biologist in me is thrilled at examining the intricate system of undulating tube feet on its ventral side!

### 11. Recognize their birthdays.

I've known teachers who have all kinds of creative ways of recognizing students' birthdays. My method was actually very simple. My early morning ritual when I arrived at school included checking to see if any of my students had a birthday that day or, if it was a Friday, if anyone had a birthday during the upcoming weekend. As soon as the bell would ring to start class, after my usual "Happy Monday (*or Tuesday, or Wednesday . . .*)!" I would say to the student, "Happy Birthday!" and to the class I would announce, "Okay! Let's show (*insert student's name here*) some love! I'll leave the door open so we can rock the hallway on this floor!" The kids enjoyed and appreciated it when I led the class in loud, off-key birthday wishes! Sometimes the littlest gestures can make the biggest difference.

### 12. Praise students in public, but scold them in private. *NEVER* yell.

A very wise, experienced elementary school teacher taught me a long time ago, "When you yell, you lose. If you yell, you've demonstrated to the kids that you've lost control and respect for them." Now of course, you'll have to raise your voice now and then if, for example, you're teaching a physical education class outdoors or in a noisy gym, just to be heard. You might have to raise your voice to stop a kid in their tracks if you see them pursuing an action that might lead to their harm, or that might endanger other students around them. (*Think chemistry lab, where a student is about to mix the wrong chemicals, or in an industrial technology class, where students are incorrectly using a table saw.*) What I'm talking about here is reprimanding or disciplining the student who has a behavior problem. I've never viewed myself as the greatest disciplinarian, so I chose to use what I call preventive discipline. In other words, set up a learning environment that is such an attention-grabber, so interesting, so engaging, (*and yes, maybe even fun*) that the students won't have the time or the desire to misbehave (*Recall, "Mr. Ruhl, I like biology because we get to do stuff in here!"*). Now, of course, occasionally I would have that kid, who would still manage to find a way to act inappropriately. I learned that if I confronted that student in front of the whole class, he felt, knowing that his peers were watching, obliged to "save face" and demonstrate a defiant, argumentative attitude. As a teacher, it's next to impossible to win in that scenario. I found it best to calmly say, without emotion, something very brief and firm such as, "(*Insert name of student here.*), please (*notice the good manners modeling going on here?*) come and see me when we split up and begin the day's activities after these announcements. I want to chat for a minute." As the students got up from their seats and began moving to their work stations, I would look down at some papers I was holding while the culprit slowly and cautiously—*What's Mr. Ruhl going to do to me?*—walked up towards me. I would look up from that stack of papers and say something like, "Oh. Yes. I just wanted to chat with you for a minute. I know you have a lot of work to do, so it won't take long." We would then step outside the open door of the classroom, out of earshot, with the student out of sight of the other kids and me positioning myself so I could "keep one eye on the class." In those situations, reminding myself to be firm, friendly, and fair, I found that even the most annoying kid, without an audience, would act like a human being, carry on a respectful conversation with me, and come away knowing, in no uncertain terms, what my expectations were going forward.

**13. Say "hello" when you see them outside of class in the hall during passing periods, in the lunchroom, or at after-school events. Smile and act like you're genuinely happy to see them.**

This one is so easy to do! But, as teachers, in our time-pressured, busy day this gesture sometimes requires us to be intentional about it. As mentioned before, a smile is a universal expression of warmth and acceptance and it can be one of your most effective tools. I've always counseled my young student teachers, "Just be a person." It's amazing how something as simple as a smile can communicate to students that you care.

**14. Attend their after-school extracurricular events.**

Whenever possible, this one is a must do! Kids will notice when you show up at their choir or band concerts, musicals or plays, science fairs or athletic events, and when you do, they will perceive that you genuinely care about them. Carving out time for such activities can be extremely difficult, given a teacher's busy professional and personal schedule, but I'm sure you will find that the time invested in attending at least a few of your students' outside-of-class events will result in increased student motivation and improved behavior in class.

One day not long ago, I had heard that our girls' high school softball team would be having a home game after school, so I thought I would go, since several of my students were on the team. I made my way up the bleachers and found a seat above our home team's dugout along the third baseline. It wasn't long before I saw a student's head pop up and look up into the stands and then pop right back down again. A few moments later, I heard a voice in the dugout: "Mr. Ruhl came to our game!" I'm convinced that if you take the time to attend at least a few of their outside-of-class activities, that it will pay off. Having first-hand experience witnessing their home run, their solo in the school musical, their last second shot in the basketball game, or their marching band show during halftime of the football game, will give you even more material that you can use when you strike up those short relationship-building conversations in the lunchroom, in the hallway, or as the students trickle into your classroom before or shortly after the bell rings.

In our teacher training courses in college and then in teacher professional development meetings at the beginning of the school year or in faculty meetings during the school year, we learn a great deal about research-based teaching techniques. Don't get me wrong, learning about and building a repertoire of teaching techniques is important as we strive to continue honing our skills, but my experience has taught me that the most important and often overlooked teaching technique is simply showing the kids that you care. It's not new or complicated. For thousands of years throughout human history and even pre-history, the greatest teachers who ever lived knew the importance of building relationships and demonstrating love for their students or their disciples. An air-tight lesson plan is important. A well-organized, consistent discipline plan is important. Effective use of technology is important. The standards are important (*but please don't let them stifle your creativity!*). However, what students will remember most is that you took an interest in them and that you asked them about their extracurricular activities, hobbies, or part-time jobs. What they will remember most is that you simply said hello to them in the hall. What they will remember most is that you remembered their birthdays. What they will remember most is that you were transparent, real, and had the ability to laugh at yourself, and to laugh with them. What the kids will remember most of all is *you*. Long after they've left your class and graduated, what the students will remember most will be the passion you demonstrated for what you were teaching; passion that grabbed their attention, motivated them, and maybe even inspired them. Some of the unforeseen rewards of having taught for four decades are the occasional thank you letters, emails, or Facebook messages from former students that read something like this: "Mr. Ruhl, do you remember me? It's been a long time! You won't believe this but because you loved teaching us so much, and you were so passionate about biology, you got my attention and so I am now a—*some of the letters read 'genetic counselor, or doctor, or wild-life biologist, or nurse, or teacher'.*" Talk about bringing on happy tears in this retired teacher! Not all the tears have been happy, though. I have an old letter in my file from a young woman, whom I still think about from time to time. In this letter, she talked about how she never felt that she was "good at science," but her guidance counselor had encouraged her to take my human genetics class. She wrote that she never did end up going to college, but that her husband did and he was working as an electrical engineer. As I read on, tears began to flow and they weren't exactly of the happy variety. No, these tears resulted from a paradoxical mix of heartache and joy. I guess I would classify them as "mixed feelings kinds of tears." As the letter continued, I learned that she and her husband were grieving the loss of their first baby that sadly, was stillborn. Paraphrasing her letter, she went on to write, "They found out that our baby had Trisomy-18, a chromosomal disorder that I remembered learning about in your class. My husband was devastated. He really took it hard. He wondered if the loss of our baby was somehow our fault. Was it something we did wrong, or didn't do right? Was God punishing us? Does this run in the family and could this happen again? Even though he went to college, he never had much training in biology, so he had never heard about chromosomes in general or Trisomy-18 in particular. So, I sat down with him, and with pencil and paper, I showed him how meiosis works—how Mom and Dad split up copies of their chromosomes and distribute them to the baby, and how sometimes a mistake happens, accidentally producing a sperm or an egg with an extra chromosome (*in our case, from chromosome pair number 18*). I explained to him how it generally doesn't run in families at all; that it's just a random accident of meiosis that can happen to anyone anytime. I shared how you showed us the data that demonstrates that 50 percent of all miscarriages and stillbirths are due to the baby having the wrong number of chromosomes due to such accidents in meiosis. You know, Mr. Ruhl, it didn't take away all his pain, but it sure helped him a lot! It certainly eased his mind. So, I just wanted to say thank you, Mr. Ruhl! Even though I wasn't the best student (*I really struggled for my grades*), what I learned helped me to help my husband. . ." That letter stunned me and reminded me that we can never tell how much of an impact we might have on our students, and how important it is to handle our students with care.

If you're a high school or college student and you feel drawn to a career in teaching, you'll hear people telling you things like, "Well, you can't make a lot of money in teaching. You'd do a lot better in business or industry. Kids these days just don't want to learn. There are too many restrictions and roadblocks being enacted by non-educators in state legislatures that place too many extra non-teaching tasks and responsibilities on teachers." But I encourage you to listen also to the voices of educators like myself. Take it from me. Teaching is a noble profession because it is a profession that will allow you to make a real difference in the world, by enriching the lives of others. The rewards from realizing that you've left a small piece of the world a little better than you found it and of the relationships with people—present and former students—that you have established, far surpass the rewards of accumulating riches that "you can't take with you."

# CHAPTER 4

# Life Lessons I've Learned as a Teacher

Teachers love learning and I would have to say that over the years, I've probably learned more important life lessons from my students, colleagues, and yes, even critters in my biology classroom, than they have from me—life lessons that I think, over time, helped me to develop into a better teacher.

**Lesson #1 – Be Willing to Make Yourself Vulnerable (Be a person!)**

Anyone who has raised or worked with teenagers knows that adolescence can be a confusing, tumultuous, traumatic, dramatic, and yet joyous and exciting period of childhood and adulthood happening all at the same time. It can be quite challenging for a teacher of teens because any student can alternate between being a responsible adult one day and exhibiting childish behavior the next day. As a high school teacher, I've always admired the teachers of middle and junior high school-aged students. They work with classrooms full of four different species of students—pre-pubescent females, post-pubescent females, pre-pubescent males, and post-pubescent males! When those kids became ninth graders (*some of them still pretty "squirrely"*) and entered my biology class, the skills that I learned from those middle and junior high teachers certainly helped me, *at least a little.*

Kids can put up a good front. A kid's outward appearance and behavior can be misleading. Deep down inside the high school stud, star football player who swaggers into the classroom, there is a vulnerable, insecure child. If the layers of the popular homecoming queen could be peeled away, you would find a child with secret insecurities and doubts as well. Living in the present throes of adolescence, teens don't have the benefit of knowing what it's like to be an adult looking back with humorous nostalgia on those awkward years of life. And I've noticed that, too often, with all the secret doubts and insecurities that teens harbor within themselves, they tend to view adults in positions of authority as persons who "have it all together." One of the best "ice breakers" I've stumbled upon is storytelling—one of the oldest and most effective teaching techniques. I remember how the kids enjoyed the times when I would share personal, humorous blunders from my own high school years, and the lessons that they taught me. Somehow, kids who are painfully aware of their own flaws are encouraged to find that their teacher is a real person as well, and relieved to learn that there really is life after high school. I believe that when the students can see that their teacher is willing to "be a good sport" and make themselves vulnerable, it can go a long way toward strengthening the relationship between teacher and students that is so vital to effective teaching and learning. I learned this by accident during the first couple weeks of the first year of my teaching career. As I described in Chapter 3, I was the new (*the lunch ladies serving in the cafeteria thought I was a student at first!*) biology teacher in a large inner-city school in Macon, Georgia. Oh, how insecure and scared I felt! I remember telling myself, "Ooze confidence, even if you have to fake it!" If you've ever been a first-year teacher, I know you'll understand. As I recall, it was the second day of school and one of my African American students, Carl, a 6'2" varsity basketball stand-out, playfully challenged me to a one-on-one basketball game after school one day that week. As I remember, I said something like, "Yeah, that might be fun . . ." (*What was I thinking?!*) I thought he might lose interest but no! He brought it up again the next day! So, I gave in. I told him, "Maybe, after school tomorrow.

*Maybe. We'll see."* I think I said to myself, "Self! Can't you just say 'no'?" Carl had a cheerful, engaging personality, a ready smile, and a long athletic body with a swagger to go along with it. I remember like it was yesterday. The hallways were empty because it was about a half-hour after school had let out for the day. Some of the students, Carl included, had seen me some days after school working out in the weight room, so he knew I had gym clothes that I changed into after school. On that fateful day, as I was walking back to my classroom after having checked my mailbox in the high school office, Carl appeared. "Hey, Mr. Ruhl, you ready? Go get changed into your gym clothes!" I think my heart skipped a beat. Looking back, I really think the decision I made that day might have been a turning point in my career. It was probably only nanoseconds, but it seemed like forever as I waffled back-and-forth in my mind wondering whether to take Carl up on his challenge. With unconscious will, I muttered, "Okay. See you in the gym." After changing clothes, I made my way to the gym and there he was, waiting for me at the door, spinning the basketball on his forefinger. Somehow, he looked even taller! We bounce-passed the ball back-and-forth to each other as we walked out onto the gym floor towards one end of the court. I heard a murmur of what sounded like a multitude, that slowly grew into a deafening crescendo of stomping, rhythmic clapping. I turned around and was horrified to see the balcony full of hundreds of grinning, enthusiastic students, who had turned up to witness this newcomer from Indiana challenge Carl, the popular, battle-tested champion of the gladiator arena! I knew that I was as good as dead, but I also knew that maybe I could at least put up a respectable fight. I had been an athlete, having played football and baseball all through high school. I only stuck with basketball up through the ninth grade, but I played in plenty of pick-up basketball games, especially in the co-recreational gym at Purdue in my undergraduate days. As a young, twenty-one-year-old teacher, I was in pretty good shape at that time, so I even flirted with the thought that maybe I had a chance (*maybe one in ten? No, out of the question!*) Carl and I stepped to the half-court line as the stomping and clapping in the balcony rose to a deafening level. He leaned towards me since it was a bit difficult to hear one another. He clarified the rules. We would only play half-court (*thank God!*). After a player made a basket, we would walk back to the top of the key and it would be the other player's turn with the ball. If the ball hit the rim and the non-shooting opponent grabbed the rebound, he had to take it back to the top of the key beyond the foul line before going to the basket again. We would play to twenty-one, with each basket counting one point. The winner had to win by two, so if there was a tie, for example, 21–21, play would continue until one player had gained a two-point lead. Carl let me have the ball first. As I stood, ball in hand at the top of the key, fear set in, and with that fear, a surge of adrenalin. Many times, in the world of sports, the excitement and adrenaline can, in a mysterious way, enable an underdog to play "out of his mind and over his head." We've all heard incredible accounts of the effects of adrenalin enabling people to perform almost super-human feats when under extreme stress, such as a woman who managed to lift the back end of a wrecked car off her husband, who had been pinned underneath its weight. I think that's what happened during that one-on-one basketball game back in the fall of 1978. I peered through Carl's long outstretched arms and fingers, and at first, I couldn't see the basket very well because his fingers blocked most of my view. Since I was 5'10", he had a height advantage on me! I thought, "Let's just go for broke!" So, I shot-faked once and launched, from the top of the key, what, by today's rules would be a deep three-pointer. Much to my shock, it swished! Nothing but net! In all honesty, a lucky shot. The kids in the bleachers went wild with cheering! Adrenalin continued to surge as I pushed my body to the limits during that contest. I think my lungs continued to burn for the rest of that day and into the evening hours! When Carl got the ball after that first shot, he drove to the basket and despite my best defensive effort, scored with a layup that I know he must have made look easy. Then it was my turn again. Starting at the top of the key, I thought, "Okay. This time I'll fake up with a shot and drive around him for a reverse lay-up. That strategy worked, at least up until I released the ball with a cocky finger roll, which he not only blocked, but swatted into the bleachers! Yes, a dose of humility can be good now and then, I guess. That whole game was a battle. Carl was blessed with a long, athletic body and height advantage (*and skill!*). I probably had a bit more upper body strength so I had to depend more on being physical, especially when it came to blocking out and rebounding. If we would have had a referee, I probably would have fouled out, but anybody who knows basketball, knows that when opposing centers are jockeying for position and posting up in the paint, it's anything *but* a noncontact sport! My adrenalin continued to surge as I played "over my head," making shots that really had no business going in. It was a contest reminiscent of the first *Rocky* movie where the challenger, Rocky Balboa went the distance with the champ, Apollo Creed.[1] Our score was tied almost the entire game as we fought towards a final score of twenty-one, with each basket being worth one point. In the end, Carl was victorious, finally beating me in overtime by a couple baskets. His victory was entirely predictable, and most importantly, appropriate. The kids in the balcony stood and cheered wildly as Carl gave me a bro-hug! The next morning, when I walked into the school building, I was greeted by smiling, enthusiastic students, some of whom extended handshakes, pats on the back, and exclamations of "Dawg, Mr. Ruhl! I didn't know you could play *ball!*" I had earned the students' respect. And it wasn't because of basketball skill. I think it was simply because I was willing to be a good sport. From that day forward, the challenges of classroom management seemed to be so much easier, and that first year of teaching turned out to be most memorable, enjoyable, and rewarding. Each teacher is a unique individual, and so each teacher must find their own unique way of making connections and establishing relationship with their students. For me, it was that basketball game. I sometimes wonder how that first year might have gone, if I had turned down Carl's one-on-one challenge. Would I have survived that first year? Would I have stayed in teaching? Who knows? What I do know is that I learned an important lesson that day: Be a real person. Be a good sport, and don't be afraid to allow yourself to be vulnerable.

## Lesson #2 – Be Compassionate (Be a person!)

Much like the nursing profession, teaching requires a unique mix of grit or toughness, and compassion. First let's look at the grit part. Why is this toughness important? There are several reasons. All veteran teachers are familiar with the tiring, long, after-contract hours; uncompensated work that must be devoted to lesson planning and grading. Add to that the number of extra responsibilities that seem to be added to teachers' plates each year—additional expectations that they never told us about in those college teacher preparation courses: how to be a counselor, policeman, child psychologist, detective, fund raiser, negotiator, mediator, nurse, secretary, equipment repairman, social events coordinator, public relations person, and social worker. Grit is essential for developing the "thick skin" needed for surviving the hurtful insults and disrespect that the occasional troubled teen can direct towards the teacher (*and even the disrespect that some adults can demonstrate towards our profession*). It's been said that "Toddlers will step on your toes and teenagers will step on your heart."[2] I remember the advice that a college professor gave me before I started student-teaching: "When a kid misbehaves or disrespects you, don't take it personally." As teachers, if we're honest, we all know that's easier said than done! The "head" will acknowledge that in most cases, insults and behavioral problems stem from problems at home and/or because of the natural, rebellious-leaning tendency that comes with adolescence, but the "heart" of the teacher can still be bruised. The heart of a teacher is especially susceptible, because it is a teacher's heart for kids that led to the decision to become a teacher in the first place.

Now for the all-important compassion part. Why is compassion important in teaching? I'm convinced it's important because the human brain is wired for loving and being loved, and even the most difficult kids can be "won over" if they perceive that their teacher genuinely cares about them, as I've already mentioned. Establishing a positive relationship with a challenging or "at-risk" student, who has sadly learned not to trust adults, can sometimes take a long time. For the last thirty-six years of teaching,

I taught in a large urban school so we had seven biology teachers in the science department. Because of the computerized scheduling and seemingly random shuffling that took place during the semester break, there was no guarantee that I would have the same students in both the fall and spring semesters. I remember the frustration that I felt when finally, by the end of the fall semester, I had broken through and established a successful relationship with a troubled student—who had finally started experiencing success in my class— only to discover at the beginning of the spring semester that the student had been transferred to another biology teacher for the spring semester. I confess that it may have been selfish on my part but it *would* have been much easier to have the same students both semesters.

As I've said before, I learned a great deal about the importance of compassion in teaching from elementary teachers and special education teachers. I also learned it from many students over the years, and there's one particular lesson that I will remember forever. It was in the spring of 1987. My wife, Gail and I had a precious little three-year-old daughter, Alison (*who has always been a beautiful nurturer, now a successful businesswoman, a wife to our wonderful son-in-law Will Wade, and mother to two adorable daughters—Mollyann and Abigail*), who was eagerly anticipating the arrival of our second child. Gail and I were, of course, ecstatic because infertility is defined as not being able to get pregnant after one year of unprotected sex, and we had tried for two years to conceive. Suddenly the miscarriage happened on a dark and devastating night of anguish that I'll never forget. I remember sitting on the step outside the back door of the house with Alison a couple days later, explaining to her, as best I could, why "the baby died inside Mommy's tummy." That was one of the most difficult conversations I've ever had with another human being, because not only was she very sad, but she was confused, having prayed with genuine child-like faith for that baby. The talk was made even more difficult because I too had struggled to understand the loss. I vacillated between the "head" and the "heart" as I struggled to make sense of what had happened. In my private moments, my "heart" cried out to God, "Why!?" Then, as a genetics teacher in a junior-senior level biology elective that focused a great deal on medical genetics and bioethics, my "head" reminded me that 50 percent of miscarriages are due to the fetus having the wrong number of chromosomes; accidents of meiosis. But then again, the anguished "heart" would cry out: "But why did it have to have the wrong number of chromosomes?" (*Little did we know, that three years later, we would be blessed with a son, Patrick, who is now a wildlife biology professor at Harding University in Searcy, Arkansas, husband to our incredible daughter-in-law Jen, and father to two little boys— Dean and Silas!*)

So how did my students teach me about compassion? It happened a couple days after our family's loss. It was time for me to drag myself back to school. The usual dread of having to "pick up the pieces left by my absence" paled in comparison to the dread I felt for the lesson that I would be teaching that day in my ninth grade biology classes—a lesson that I normally thoroughly enjoyed. It was early enough in my career that I was still lecturing quite a bit, and it was time in my carefully planned curriculum to share with the students the details of human embryo development. As a biologist, I've always marveled at the beautiful complexities of embryology and the turning off and on of different arrays of genes resulting in cell differentiation. I have always loved sharing with my students the wonders of this "miracle of life"—how a single fertilized egg cell, no bigger than a barely visible pencil dot on paper, is able to develop into a ¾-inch-long fetus with completely developed organs in just forty-nine days. But as I put one foot in front of the other, willing my way through the dark, quiet hallways a couple hours before the students arrived, my usual enthusiasm was lacking. How was I going to do this? Would I be able to "bring it?" Should I resort to some other lesson for the day? Or should I "buck up" and just do it? I opted for continuing the lesson as planned because, quite honestly, it would have been more difficult to change the plans I had, and besides, the students were enjoying this unit of study. Incredibly, the day, bolstered by private prayer time, turned out to be one of those "fake it until you make it" days (*remember Chapter 3?*). My enthusiasm for the subject soon became genuine in all three of my biology classes as I projected slides of those beautiful, stunning Lennart Nilsson photos of the stages of human embryo development.[3] I'll never forget those kids that day. They were not the usual immature ninth graders. They were like the most attentive, polite, note-taking, adult graduate students in some seminary! In many of the students' eyes that day, I saw genuine human empathy with an occasional subtle, supportive smile as I led them through the lesson. You know that look of encouragement that some listeners will give to a public speaker? I remember thinking, "Word travels fast in a school community. They know why Mr. Ruhl has been gone for the last two days." Because of their help, in all three classes, it turned out to be one of those "home run" lessons, even in the third period class. Third period was that one class that every teacher seems to have. It was normally the most immature, annoying, irritating, most difficult to motivate of the three classes. It was the class that struggled the most academically. But on this day, they were dramatically different, and what happened at the end of that third period class floored me. After we dismissed and the bell rang to proceed to fourth period, a few of the kids, without a word, hugged me on the way out, even the big, macho, stoic football player. Remember, we're talking about high school kids now! My kids at school taught me an important lesson about compassion and the power of love that day. Paradoxically, it was one of the hardest days of my teaching career, but also, one of the best.

## Lesson #3 – Embrace Those Lessons in Humility and Learn from Them

In life there seem to be more failures than successes, and that's why the occasional wins or successes are so sweet. The same is true in teaching. Like every teacher who has ever lived, I've had my share of failures. I haven't always presented lessons that inspired the students. I haven't always responded appropriately to the troublemaker. But the important thing to do after any setback or humiliating experience is to pick yourself up, dust yourself off, reflect on what went wrong, and learn from it. When I first started out as a young, beginning teacher, my classroom management skills were dismal and many lessons just flopped, but I vowed to myself that I would strive to learn from the mistakes. Each year, I worked to be a more effective teacher than I was the year before. Even up until the day I retired, I felt like I was still learning! So how do we keep learning? First, since "none of us is as smart as all of us," (Ken Blanchard) seek out veteran teacher colleagues in your school who are respected and successful. Listen to them and if they're open to it, observe parts of their classes during your prep time and "pick their brains." Learn from those who have "learned the ropes." If possible, have an administrator or willing veteran teacher observe one of your classes and offer feedback to you. Actually, administrators are now required to make periodic observations. As a teacher, in order to be a life-long learner, one must accept and embrace a spirit of humility—an attitude of "I've got a lot to learn." I know it's easier said than done, but we must strive to set our egos aside when receiving *constructive* criticism. Secondly, in those mandatory professional development meetings in your school, don't sit in the back with the gripers and paper graders, but sincerely seek to learn at least one new idea or technique that could help you to become a better teacher. Thirdly, join your professional organization(s), read their journals, and whenever possible, attend their conventions or professional development meetings to pick up tried and tested tips and techniques from the best teachers "in the trenches." Joining professional organizations and attending their conferences can be a sacrifice financially, but I found it to be vital to my professional growth. Sometimes, depending on the school system that you work in, you can even get some or even all your trip reimbursed by your administration. In fact, during your interview when applying for a teaching position, the interviewer will always ask, "Now, what questions do you have for us?" That's when you can ask, "What kind of support is there for teachers who seek to improve themselves by attending professional development conferences?" As a science teacher, I found that attending conventions of the National Science Teaching Association (NSTA), National Association of Biology Teachers (NABT), and the Hoosier Association of Science Teachers, Inc. (HASTI), inspired and invigorated me, and provided me with a wealth of new and exciting, ready-to-implement teaching strategies. Strolling through the exhibit halls at those conferences, I was able to pick up all kinds of "freebies" such as eye-catching, instructive posters that I could decorate my classroom with in my efforts to create an inviting, interesting environment for both my students *and* myself. And many times, I picked up the best ideas simply by talking to other teachers in the hallways between sessions.

As I've mentioned, in order to be a growing, life-long learner as a teacher, one must accept and embrace a spirit of humility. One of the strangest, most bizarre lessons in humility was taught to me not by my students, teacher colleagues, or administrators, but by a large classroom pet—a green iguana named "Iggy." As a biology teacher, I enjoyed maintaining a classroom environment that was both a zoo and a museum. The students loved it and found it to be motivating. Iggy was one of the creatures in our classroom zoo, who had grown to a fairly large size of about eighteen inches in length, not counting his tail, which added on another twenty-seven inches. He had reached the stage where he had become a sexually mature male with an "attitude" (*not unlike some humans I've observed during passing periods in the school hallways!*). I had noticed that when approached, he would sometimes display territorial behavior such as quick, little head-bobbing movements, which told me it was time to stop allowing the students to hold him. In fact, I had gotten to the point where I would put one hand on his back before reaching for his food or water dish with the other hand. That fateful day when Iggy taught me humility is a memory (and a visible reminder) that I will carry with me forever! It was early in the fall and the educational process in our school was shut down for a week as we all engaged in state-mandated standardized testing, despised by both students and faculty. In fact, every school in the state of Indiana was required to participate. I was proctoring the test in another classroom downstairs with a group of students I did not know. Another teacher, who was assigned to give me a scheduled break, appeared at the appointed time, so I thought I would take advantage of that free time and go upstairs to my classroom (*which was empty of students and not being used as a testing room because it was deemed to be an environment too distracting for testing*) to feed and water a few of the animals. I remember going over to Iggy's cage and opening the cage door. Accidents always seem to happen when we're in a hurry and that was the case in this life-changing moment. I knew my test proctoring break was short, so I reached for Iggy's food dish with my dominant, right hand without first placing my left hand on Iggy's back as was my usual practice. As I grabbed the food dish, Iggy, in a flash, lunged for my hand and clamped down on my little finger. I knew that iguanas have sharp, little serrated teeth and I learned in that agonizing moment that they also have very strong jaws! With my left hand, I picked Iggy up while he stubbornly continued to tighten his grip further. Blood immediately began running down my forearm and I observed a frightening view of the internal anatomy of my little finger as I peered into the small gap between his upper and lower jaw. It was impossible to get him to release his grip on me! I realized I was in trouble and that I might lose my finger. Oddly enough, my first thought was "I've got papers to grade and lessons to prepare! I don't have time for this!" I'm glad the students weren't in the classroom because what happened in the next couple minutes must have looked like a professional wrestling match as I tried, in vain, all kinds of moves such as mandible clawing with my free left hand, pile drivers and body slams (*trust me, I'm exaggerating the struggle a bit and I don't really watch professional wrestling!*) in order to get Iggy to release his vise-like grip. During this wrestling match, I remember thinking, "I'm so sorry Iggy. It's either you or my little finger." I don't know how or why, but after a minute or two, he eventually let go. I tossed him back into the cage, locked the door, and looked on in horror at my finger. I tried in vain to flex and straighten it, so I knew the tendons had been severed. *Great! Surgery and rehab, and I don't have time for this!* I wobbled over to the sink and ran water over my hand as it was bleeding profusely. Instinctively, I wrapped my finger with some paper towel and briskly walked down the hall and downstairs to the nurse's office. There she was, Helen Sunkel, looking like an angel of mercy as she dealt with one student after another—some who were merely hall walkers trying to get out of class, and some who were legitimately sick. She was tending to a student who supposedly had a headache when she looked up at me as I entered the room. I held up my hand, covered with the bloody towel, and announced in a faked, calm, professional tone, "I think I'm going to lose my finger." Her eyes widened and I learned about battlefield hospital triage as she dropped everything and started tending to me. The next thing I knew, the nurse's secretary leaned down and told me that an ambulance was on the way. Again, my thought (*I know it sounds odd*) was, "I don't have time for this!" As I sat waiting for the ambulance, I was overcome by an unexplainable sensation of calm. I was mildly amused when a school security guard breathlessly entered the room and shouted, "There's a blood trail all the way down the hall. What happened?" A few minutes later, after an ambulance ride to the hospital (*which created quite a stir of excitement throughout the school*), I found myself being tended to by wonderful doctors and nurses in the ER. They immediately began pumping antibiotics into me, along with the explanation that exotic reptiles can sometimes carry strange, rare, flesh-eating bacteria in their mouths—a revelation that caused a bit of consternation, at least until the pain killer they administered started to take effect. Through the ensuing mental fog, I remember someone saying, "There's a hand surgeon coming and we do have a surgical room available." As the drugs took effect, it was hard to focus my thoughts, but I do remember thinking, "Surgery? This is more serious than I thought." Through the haze, I remember climbing onto a gurney and being wheeled down to surgery. In what seemed like an instant later (*actually, the surgery lasted three hours and involved microsurgery as the hand surgeon worked to repair tiny, delicate tendons that had been severed.*), I woke up with a huge padded paddle covering my right hand. They replaced that paddle with a removeable, soft, cast-like contraption made of bandages and Velcro, that kept my fingers in a relaxed position designed to take tension off the tendons. I remember thinking, "I'm involved in hands-on lab work with my students. I write with my right hand! How am I going to do this? Will I be able to throw batting practice to my little boy?"

It wasn't long before I found myself being pushed in a wheelchair down the sidewalk to the rehab center, where I learned that I would be scheduled for physical therapy sessions during which I would be taught how to take the contraption off my hand to do simple hand exercises every two hours in order to keep the tendons flexible and to prevent them from shrinking and ultimately becoming useless. (*What?!*) I know this will sound very strange to a non-biologist, but I was quite fascinated to look at my hand and see that my little finger and the ring finger next to it were discolored and swollen to twice their normal size. I counted sixty-five tiny stitches on the outside of the finger and who knows how many on the inside! When I returned to the classroom a couple days later, the students again taught me a great deal about the power of compassion. Kids "wear their emotions on their sleeves," and the empathy, patience, and helpfulness they exhibited really touched my heart (*"Wait Mr. Ruhl. Let me help you with that. . ."*). Some kids are sometimes annoying, but most of the time, they're awesome. In every class that first day back, the conversations went something like this:

Students: "Mr. Ruhl, where's Iggy now?"

Me: "Iggy's doing just fine. He and I both survived, and he's now living at the West Lafayette Exotic Animal Shelter, where he's surrounded by 'adoring' female iguanas."

Students: "Mr. Ruhl, did you cry? Did you scream? Did you cuss?"

Me: "No, I didn't cry, scream, or cuss. But I do remember gritting me teeth and muttering, 'Ow! Ow! Iggy! Let go! Let go!'"

Students: "Why did Iggy bite your finger? He's so mean!"

Me: "Oh no. Iggy's not a monster. His reptilian brain is not capable of meanness. He simply reacted instinctively to an intruder invading his territory." (*A quick, little teachable moment about the anatomical differences between mammalian and reptilian brains!*)

During the ensuing *eighteen weeks of rehab and healing*, I had been given a powerful life lesson in humility, humbled by an iguana and my own split-second act of carelessness! Humbled, because for the rest of that semester, I was physically unable to do routine tasks. I couldn't be the teacher I wanted to be, because I was quite limited in my efforts to help students in the lab. Writing comments on the students' papers during grading sessions with my left hand was excruciating and extremely time-consuming. Whenever I wrote on the board during class, my students and I were, shall I say, quite amused by my preschool-like scrawling! With this lesson in humility, I gained a deeper sense of empathy and appreciation for, as well as patience with the struggles that many of our special needs students and adults have. I realized that my *temporary* handicap was absolutely nothing compared to the *permanent* physical and mental challenges that many of our special needs students face with optimism, courage, and resolve. I became more conscious of the daily instruction provided by our special education teachers. Those teachers probably don't realize it, but I learned a great deal about patience and compassion from them, as well as from my own students. I find myself feeling strangely thankful for that difficult semester and its lessons that made me a more compassionate and patient teacher.

I'm happy to say, I was able to keep my little finger. It's a little crooked, but I can still use it, *somewhat*. In fact, I don't really notice much limitation at all. But the famous "Iggy Affair" left an indelible mark in the annals of the history of Jefferson High School! To this day, I'll occasionally run into a former student (*and just the other day—the school nurse!*) from twenty years ago or so, who will ask, "How's your finger? Whatever happened to Iggy?"

### Lesson #4 – Be a Positive Encourager

After my first year of teaching, I left Macon, Georgia, and returned to my home in Indiana with a plan to find a teaching position as close to Purdue University as possible. Why? Because I fell in love. I was involved in a long-distance romance with a young lady, whom I had met in graduate school the summer before I took the job in Georgia. Gail Evans, a Cornell University graduate, who had completed her master's degree at Purdue

University in Botany and Plant Pathology, had just been hired at Purdue as their plant disease diagnostician and first Director of a Plant Disease and Weed Identification Clinic. (*Gail recently retired after 40 years at Purdue, and by the way, we've been married now for 41 years!*). So, I packed up my scant worldly possessions, moved back to Indiana, and landed a job at LaCrosse High School in LaCrosse, Indiana. LaCrosse is a tiny, close-knit community about seven miles south of U.S. 30, a main highway that runs across the top of northern Indiana. The town was not much more than a railroad crossing with a small grocery store, a grain elevator, a diner, a gas station, a church, a couple of bars, and the friendliest people you'll ever meet. If you drive north on U.S. 421, headed up towards the Michigan line and blink, you'll miss the town! LaCrosse High School was very different from Central High School in Macon, Georgia. Central High School was a large, inner-city school. LaCrosse, on the other hand, was a tiny, rural, ethnically homogenous Indiana school of one hundred and fifty white students in the *upper four grades*. In fact, grades one through twelve were all housed in one, three-story, brick school building that was built in 1915. My biology classroom (*which I shared with a world language teacher when she wasn't teaching in there*) was in the basement, across from the boiler/furnace room that doubled as the teacher's lounge. Remember Ralphie's old school building in the holiday classic movie, *A Christmas Story*?[4] That's the kind of old school building I'm talking about. If you've ever seen the inspiring basketball movie, *Hoosiers,* starring Gene Hackman and Barbara Hershey, you'll get a good feel for this old style of school building.[5]

LaCrosse School—grades one through twelve were all housed in one, three-story, brick school building that was built in 1915.

I remember being overwhelmed by a feeling of nostalgia and memories of my own elementary school days as I climbed the creaky stairs and admired the beautifully polished wood floors of that grand old building. Teaching materials and equipment were scarce, and so, as the lone biology teacher, I scrounged the woods and streams for specimens and frequented garage sales to acquire cages and aquariums.

As one of very few male faculty members in the high school, I had a feeling that I would be tapped for coaching athletic extracurricular activities that I was not adequately prepared to handle. Sure enough, I was moved out of my comfort zone when I was invited to a meeting with the boys' varsity basketball coach and the principal in the principal's office after school on that first day of school in mid-August. As I climbed the creaky, old wooden stairs up to the third floor, I knew what this meeting was going to be all about. They needed a junior varsity boys basketball coach. I just knew it and I was scared! Why? Because I was trained to teach biology, not coach basketball! Basketball is serious business in the state of Indiana, consuming the months of October through March. Coaches not only participate in grueling hours of practices and a multitude of games, but are also "under the microscope" of public scrutiny. I dreaded this meeting because I just knew that the community would judge me for my performance as a basketball coach rather than my work as a biology teacher. When I entered the principal's office, there was the principal, Louis Ross, and the varsity coach, Terry Butler, both warm, friendly, outstanding educators, who obviously loved kids and teaching. After brief pleasantries, we got down to business:

> Lou: "Joe, we'd like for you to be our junior varsity basketball coach for the ninth and tenth grade boys." (*I remember the rapid heartbeat and the cold sweat, despite the lack of air conditioning.*)
>
> Terry: "You would be the head coach of the junior varsity, and my assistant varsity coach, so you would assist me with the varsity practices, run your own junior varsity practices, and join me on the bench during the varsity games."
>
> Me: "Uh, I really didn't learn about coaching sports in college." (*lame response!*)
>
> Terry: "No worries! I'll teach you."
>
> Me: "Umm. Well, I played football and baseball all through high school. I only played basketball up through the ninth grade, realizing I was more cut out for football and baseball."
>
> Lou: (*smiling, obviously trying to put me at ease*) "Joe, if I held up a football and a basketball, do you think you would be able to recognize the difference between the two of them?"
>
> Me: (*a weak, faked laugh . . .*)
>
> Terry: "Congratulations! Welcome aboard! Don't worry. I'll help you!"

August and September moved along and I felt much more comfortable teaching my biology classes this second year than I did the first year. I felt like I was "getting the hang of it a little more" since I had spent a significant part of the summer reworking lesson plans that I had tried out during that first year in Georgia. Don't get me wrong. I was still very much a novice teacher, and when I think back on my classroom management skills and teaching techniques in those early years, I almost feel a need to reach out and apologize to those former students. But I've always believed that good teachers are made, not born, and I was stubbornly committed to learning from my mistakes and from my mentors, and striving each year to make my classroom and my teaching more interesting and effective than the previous year. Growing as an educator takes time, and so that's why I always advise young teachers not to decide about whether to continue their career as a teacher until they've taught for at least three years.

October rolled around and basketball practices began, so it was time to begin learning, on the job, this new role of basketball coaching on top of the all-consuming job of teaching biology. We had one gym, built in 1950 and attached to the 1915 era school building. As I mentioned previously, watch the Gene Hackman movie *Hoosiers* and the LaCrosse gym looks exactly like the one in the movie![6] During those after-school practices, I assisted Terry Butler as we coached the varsity practices from 3:30 until 5:30. I listened and watched intensely to learn the practice drills and plays and then I would repeat the same drills and plays in my junior varsity practice sessions that ran following the varsity practices from 5:30 until 7:30. At the end of the day, I drove through the countryside to my apartment in Hanna, Indiana, for an evening of paper grading and lesson planning. Hanna was a tiny town, sort of like LaCrosse, and my apartment was the furnished basement of a one-story house that an elderly widow and retired elementary teacher, LaVerne Sommers, rented out to me. LaVerne only charged me $50 a month and she was one of the kindest human beings that I've ever encountered. She wanted me to call her "Mom 2," which I was very happy to do. LaVerne was dating an equally sweet widower and retired farmer named Ed Marks, and many times, if I hadn't already eaten dinner at Ray's Grill in LaCrosse after basketball practices, they both would insist that I join them upstairs for leftovers from that evening's dinner. They have both since passed away, but I fondly remember them and their kindness, as they were just like family, and treated me like a son.

I must confess that as those basketball practices started up, initially, I faked the enthusiasm for this extra time-consuming work, but then when I saw how important basketball was to my ninth and tenth grade boys as well as their classmates and fans, it didn't take long before I realized that I needed an attitude adjustment. I remember saying something to myself like this: "Self, get out of yourself. You need an attitude adjustment! School work is of primary importance, yes, but they're kids! Play is just as important to them as work. Basketball is important to them! This is not about you. This is for them. They're putting their all into this and you need to do the same." As I got to know the boys on the team, and as they got to know me, my love for them and my enthusiasm for the game and for coaching grew almost overnight. I wasn't that much older than the varsity players and from the very beginning, my young athletes looked up to me with a sense of respect that I felt was underserved. I enjoyed this new job and I started to really "get into it!" It was exciting and we became sort of a "band of brothers." Even before I stepped into the gym to start the first practice of the season, I vowed to myself that I would not be like some coaches I had known. I had a brief stint as a summer baseball coach for junior high boys when I was a younger college student. Baseball was a game that I had played and knew pretty well, but back then, as a college student, I unfortunately mimicked coaches I had known, who negatively yelled at and "rode" their players when they made mistakes. Now, as a more "mature" college graduate and second year teacher, I was bound and determined not to coach that way. I had learned from my mentor, Purdue Biology Education professor Dr. Jane Butler Kahle, how positive encouragement can empower and create self-confidence in a young person. During my teacher training days at Purdue, Jane would praise me for the things I did well, making me genuinely believe that I had potential. When she noticed things that I needed to work on, she didn't point them out in a "preachy" sort of way, but rather, in a way that made me feel good about my efforts. I promised myself that in those basketball practices and games, every word out of my mouth would be positive! It is my belief that glaring and yelling at a kid when he makes a bad pass or bounces the ball off his foot and out-of-bounds does more harm than good. Clapping when a kid makes a mistake and yelling "That's okay! Good hustle! You got this!" can do wonders. I was intentional about looking that player in the eye during a timeout and saying, "Don't worry about that. I love your hustle! What would you do differently next time?" And I was determined that my kids would never see me yelling at a referee after a call that didn't go our way. Not only did I learn about coaching basketball while on the job, but I also learned about and saw first-hand the power of positive encouragement on my players that Dr. Kahle had modeled for me. Even before the first game of that season, and even though I was growing to love the work, I still harbored a bit of resentment at having to add this extra time commitment to my already limited twenty-four-hour day and my primary responsibility of being a biology teacher—the work that I had trained for in the first place. So, my mildly rebellious nature manifested itself in my decision to run this team differently than what was commonly expected in Indiana basketball culture and tradition. There would be no showmanship on my part in the form of ranting and raving on the sidelines. I decided that every player on my bench—not just the stars—would get to play some in each game. As I've already mentioned, my every word was going to be positive and encouraging. As a result, my junior varsity team had a very successful, dominating, winning season! Many people said that our junior varsity games, played right before the main event of the varsity games, were more exciting to watch than the varsity! Many times, our subs, who came off the bench, brought us from behind in inspiring rallies as adrenalin coursed through their veins! Now I must admit, whenever I had less skillful subs in the game, I made sure to rotate through the players and keep one or two stars on the floor with them. I found myself enjoying those moments of rapid-fire, real-time problem solving and strategic decision making. What was not always easy to deal with, though, were the two fathers of my two best players. They were supportive and positive most of the time, but I do remember how the two of them would quickly walk out and through the doors that led to the gym foyer whenever I took their boys out of the game. I could see them out there, nervously pacing, muttering to one another, and puffing up a storm on their cigarettes. But I was stubborn and determined to let them all play, thankful that I was not a varsity coach faced with even more pressure to win.

My players and I became a family—something I had not even dreamed of when I agreed to coach that basketball season. I loved it! My basketball players, the junior varsity cheerleaders, and the student fans were all in my freshman biology class and my role as JV coach served to strengthen even more the positive teacher-to-students relationship that I knew was essential for effective teaching and learning. Even though it wasn't his responsibility to do so, the LaCrosse school board president approached me at the end of the school year and told me, "We would really like for you to be the varsity coach next year." I told him, "Thanks," but that I had recently accepted a job for the next school year to be the biology teacher at North White High School in Monon, Indiana—a teaching job that moved me closer to West Lafayette (and Gail at Purdue). North White High School was a small rural school as well, about twice the size of LaCrosse and located just thirty miles north of West Lafayette. In the spring when I announced to the kids that I would be moving on, they hung their heads—a painful memory for me. Three years later, though, I was blessed with what turned out to be a precious, cherished memory, as those kids, when they became seniors, invited me back to be the commencement speaker at their graduation. I ended up teaching biology and advanced biology at North White for the next four years, during which time Gail and I were married. At the end of the fourth year at North White, a biology teaching job opened at Jefferson High School in Lafayette, just across the Wabash River from Purdue University, where Gail worked as a plant disease diagnostician. Jefferson High School turned out to be my "home" for the last thirty-six years of my teaching career. Moving from LaCrosse and North White to Jeff was a major culture shock, as I was now not the lone biology teacher in a small rural school, but one of seven biology teachers in a department of sixteen science teachers within a large inner-city school of over two thousand students in grades 9–12.

So, what did accepting the new, unfamiliar challenge of coaching basketball at LaCrosse High School teach me? It taught me two valuable lessons that turned out to serve me well in the classroom for the next forty years. First, I learned not to settle for the comfortable and the routine. Take risks! Don't be afraid to try new teaching strategies! (*Check out the next chapter for a couple examples of risk-taking in teaching.*) Secondly, I learned about the power of positive encouragement. My basketball players were winners because they *believed* that they were winners, causing them at times, to "play over their heads." They believed because I tried to be intentional about encouraging them. Since I was painfully aware that I was not a brilliant coaching tactician (*My goodness, I was trained as a science teacher, not a coach!*) I was determined to make up for my lack of coaching skills by being intentional about being a positive encourager. My players believed in themselves because they knew I believed in them. This was probably the most important lesson that I learned during that basketball season. Forty-two years in the classroom has taught me that looking for (*sometimes we have to look hard!*) and praising the positives in students can bring out the best in them both in terms of their behavior and their performance.

# CHAPTER 5

# Risky Behavior

I love a quote from Dave Burgess in his book *Teach Like a Pirate*. Dave said, "Provide an uncommon experience for your students and they will reward you with an uncommon effort and attitude."[1] Providing uncommon experiences for our students can require us to move out of our comfort zone; to take risks. But taking those risks (*like agreeing to coach basketball at LaCrosse!*) can produce indescribable joy and satisfaction for both the students and the teacher, resulting in increased learning. In this chapter, I'll share a couple stories of times when I provided uncommon experiences for my students by engaging in what I'll call "extreme forms of risky behavior in the classroom."

Role-playing famous historical characters is not a new teaching technique. I've read of creative history teachers, who have dressed up and role-played as famous historical characters and even brought in guest speakers such as Abraham Lincoln impersonators or Civil War reenactors. I've always thought that could work as well in the science classroom. In fact, one of my mentors, Steve Randak, the most creative biology teacher I have ever known, did just that in his classroom decades ago. This is not a common practice in science classes throughout the country, but there are so many interesting scientists from the past that could be "resurrected" and brought in as guest speakers, so I thought, why not? Such a decision to do so was not easy for me. If I came to class dressed as a famous scientist from the past, would the kids simply laugh me out of the room? Would I lose control of my class? I did not participate in plays or musicals when I was in high school because I was too shy, and as an adult, I still lean towards the introvert end of the personality continuum. But I decided to "throw caution to the wind" and take the plunge. Who knows, it might be fun!

In 2016, Gregor Mendel, the 19th century Augustinian monk who discovered the laws of inheritance by crossing different varieties of garden pea plants, visited my classroom!

**Figure 5-1** Gregor Mendel visited my classroom!

You can watch the video of his presentation online here:

https://www.youtube.com/watch?v=Mxt9GxyE4sI&t=94s

In preparation for this unusual lesson plan, I went to a local store that rents out theater and Halloween costumes, and they kindly sold me a black monk's robe and padre priest hat, along with period glasses with flat lenses. I constructed a wooden crucifix and spray painted it silver. I even fashioned a white clerical collar by cutting the collar off an old white dress shirt, buttoning it onto my neck, and turning it around backwards! I studied up on the life and work of Gregor Mendel so I could informally talk to my students about not only the scientific work that "I" did in the mid 1860s, but also about "my life" growing up, the personal disappointments and failures that "I" suffered through and learned from, and ultimately the discovery of the basic principles of genetics that are used in agriculture, the biomedical industry, medicine, and genetic counseling today. On the day that "Mendel" visited, I arrived at school extra early so I could prepare myself for those first three class periods of the day, knowing that I would finally get a break when my fourth period prep time rolled around. It was so early, there were hardly any people in the building yet, especially students. In the boys' restroom located just outside my classroom, I plastered on gobs of hair gel so that I could slick my hair back flat, revealing a high forehead just like Mendel had! Then I sprayed my white hair with black theatrical hair dye, wondering if it would really wash out, but hey! It was all for the cause! I was in deep and now there was no turning back! I carefully donned the costume and I was ready. After students and teachers started arriving at school, I realized that I needed to head down to the teachers' mailboxes located in the school library. Because Jefferson is a large school, I managed to successfully sneak down there and back without any of my own students spotting me. I did overhear one puzzled student (*not one of mine*) in the hallway say to a friend, "I didn't know that he was priest on the side!"

A half-hour before any students arrived at my classroom, I wrote on the board "Guest Speaker – Gregor Mendel." That's all. Then I opened the classroom door, went into my office, which was conveniently attached to the classroom, shut the office door, turned off the office lights and sat in the dark, waiting for the kids to arrive. Here I was, by now a veteran teacher, but I felt more nervous during those moments than I think I did when I faced my students for the first time as a first year teacher. As I sat there, hearing the buzz and chatter of the kids along with the noisy scooting of chairs as they settled in, I tried not to think of the risk that I was taking in leaving the students somewhat unsupervised, but it would only be for a few moments. The principal came over the intercom with the usual morning announcements and I felt a sense of pride as they quieted down and listened attentively. After the principal signed off, I listened with amusement to the conversations that started up in the classroom!

"Where's Mr. Ruhl? He's always at the door."

"Do we have a sub today?"

"Oh, I hope so!"

"What should we do? Should we go get somebody?"

"No! Let's just shut the door and be quiet."

And finally, after a couple minutes of unexpected silence, one boy said, "It says 'Guest Speaker – Gregor Mendel' on the board. Isn't Gregor Mendel dead?"

I had to muffle an audible laugh at this one, because someone had *finally* noticed the board and yes, Gregor Mendel died in 1884! (*Out of the mouths of babes!*)

Finally, I slowly opened the door of my darkened office that led into the classroom, walked in with my hands piously clasped in front of me, and looked around the room as I carefully, slowly made my way to the front of the room. There was only a brief, two-second-long period of a few giggles, but then, complete silence and total, riveted attention from the students! I think they were in shock, and I remember thinking this is fun! They were most polite with this guest speaker and they even treated "Gregor Mendel" better than they treat Mr. Ruhl! I politely removed my padre priest hat, revealing the new hairdo, and of course, this elicited surprised outbursts of laughter that only lasted a few seconds, but then the students returned, just as quickly, to being politely focused again. I simply started out by saying something like, "Mr. Ruhl could not be here today and he asked me if I would be your substitute teacher. Before I tell you about my research and discoveries, what kinds of questions do you have for me?" The students, during our genetics unit, had a limited, cursory knowledge of Gregor Mendel, so they respectfully raised their hands, one at a time, and asked me things like:

"Why did you become a monk?"

"Where were you born?"

"Did you have any brothers or sisters?"

"Do monks ever do anything for fun?"

"What was it like living in the monastery?"

"What made you decide to study pea plants in your research?"

"How did you feel when all the other scientists didn't accept your ideas?"

I'll never forget how I felt as my nervousness gave way to exhilaration. As I fielded their questions, I thought, "This is so much fun! They're even playing along! Of course! Kids like make believe and play!" Storytelling, often overlooked and underutilized in science teaching, is one of the oldest and most effective teaching techniques, especially when the speaker is acting and role-playing. After their questions about "my" personal life, I transitioned into a guest lecturer, where I explained the genetics experiments "I" had done and the discoveries that "I" had made. To my amazement, the students were riveted, 100 percent on task, and taking notes for the entire ninety-minute period, even the less academically inclined! There would have been no way for me—the real Mr. Ruhl—to get away with lecturing for 90 minutes! For over an hour, it was almost as if the kids forgot that I was Mr. Ruhl. I was delighted to discover that when storytellers tell their own personal stories, then magic can happen.

As you can tell from comments I've made earlier, I loathe the idea of teaching to the test and the current politically motivated societal obsession with state-mandated standards that can stifle teacher creativity. Our state-mandated standardized testing drains the life out of teaching and learning because it consumes most of the last month of the school year, and it communicates to teachers, "You're not trusted. We need to test your students to hold you accountable. If your students don't do well, then you and your school will miss out on the limited state funds for education that we reluctantly give to schools throughout the state." Sadly, I've seen how the stress and anxiety can affect kindergarten through twelfth grade kids, as they're subjected to *several weeks* of mind-numbing testing, not to mention the prior time lost in elementary grades devoted to getting ready to take the tests. Forgive me if this rant sounds too negative. I just believe that it's more important to inspire a love of learning and to teach kids how to think, than it is to teach them how to bubble in their answer sheets with a sharpened number two pencil. Don't get me wrong. Testing, that is, *teacher-designed testing*, is important. Of course, I tested my students on Mendelian genetics each year and I kept the data on the past years' test results so I could assess my own efforts. I was excited to see that the students who sat at "Mendel's feet" did significantly better on my tests than any of the previous year's students! I firmly believe that there's magic in storytelling.

There's a postscript to this story that still tickles me when I think about it. By the end of third period, I was finished with biology classes for the day, so during my prep period I went into the boys' restroom near my classroom, took off that uncomfortable clerical collar, climbed out of the monk's robe, placed a towel over my shoulders, bent over the sink, and proceeded to wash all that dreadful gel and black dye out of my hair. Since I knew I would be covered up with a monk's robe most of the day I hadn't felt the need to dress professionally, so there I stood, hunched over the sink wearing worn blue jeans and an old white T-shirt. The halls and restrooms were mostly deserted since it *was* class time, but I heard a student slowly shuffle into the restroom. As the water ran, I turned my head slightly, squinted through the black hair dye streaming down my face, and saw a boy staring at me with eyes as big as saucers! Without taking care of business, he quickly turned and walked out of the restroom. As I've mentioned, Jefferson High School is a school of over two thousand students, so I did not know this student. Later that day, Bill Huston, a good friend and an outstanding Earth science teacher who taught down the hall, laughed when he told me that during fourth hour, one of his students had asked to leave to go to the restroom, but returned wide-eyed, sooner than expected, and urgently informed the teacher, "Mr. Huston, there's a homeless guy taking a bath in the bathroom!" Ah, those moments of serendipitous joy!

I was so encouraged by "Mendel's visit" that I thought, "Someday maybe I'll bring Charles Darwin, the most famous scientist in the history of biology, in to visit my students." In the spring of 2018, I did just that; something that I had never attempted in all the forty years of teaching up until that time. Thanks to a grant from the Public Schools foundation of Tippecanoe County, I went all out! I was able to purchase online, authentic period clothing for a gentleman from Victorian Age England, even down to the shoes. I purchased a professional quality, realistic beard, bald-cap, and make-up. I wanted to look just like the elderly, successfully published Charles Darwin near the end of his life. My schedule this particular semester was such that I was able to have my biology classes in the afternoon. So, I took a half personal day in the morning, but instead of spending it at home, I sat in the make-up room downstairs in our school's theater department. I hired a couple students who were active in the school's musicals and plays, and who were gifted in applying make-up. Those students spent two hours transforming me from Mr. Ruhl into Charles Darwin! You can watch this transformation process here:

https://www.youtube.com/watch?v=Ob1nfe1bkDc

**Figure 5-2** Charles Darwin visited my classroom!

© John Terhune – USA TODAY NETWORK

In 2005, years before "Darwin's visit," I applied for and received a generous Lilly Endowment Teacher Creativity Fellowship, which funded my eight-day excursion in the Galapagos Islands. This was a biologist's dream come true, to follow in Darwin's footprints on the exotic Pacific Islands six hundred miles west of Ecuador, where he explored, collected specimens, and took detailed notes that were instrumental in developing his theory of natural selection as the driving force of evolution. Gail was able to come along with me, thanks to a gift from her parents in celebration of her fiftieth birthday! During this eight-day Ecoventura adventure aboard a sixteen-passenger ship, in the company of two naturalist guides, we snorkeled the pristine waters around the islands, hiked the volcanic slopes, and documented the trip with video clips and photographs of the exotic plants and animals such as giant tortoises, marine iguanas, sea lions, Galapagos penguins, flightless cormorants, blue and red-footed boobies, Nazca boobies, frigate birds, waved albatross, and of course, finches that had attracted the attention of Darwin during his time on the islands. In subsequent years, I used these video clips and photographs when teaching the evolution units in my biology classes. It seemed to mean more to the students when they knew that their teacher had explored the Galapagos Islands himself, just like Darwin had. But this day in April, 2018 was special. Charles Darwin "himself" would be the storyteller. As I sat in that make-up chair, I tried to suppress my nervous jitters. Even though I had role-played Gregor Mendel years before, this role-playing was far from a routine occurrence. On top of that, since this was a locally funded grant supported project, a reporter/photographer from our local newspaper, the *Journal & Courier*, would be there along with a couple of interested administrators and a film crew. After I was made up and prepared for class, I took a little walk through the halls, which were empty because it was the middle of class time, and I had about a half hour to kill. The pacing served to calm my nerves. I did encounter a couple teachers who were on their prep period—teachers that I knew very well. It was hilarious because when they saw me, they discreetly moved to the opposite side of the hallway, averted their shocked gaze away from me, looked down at papers they were carrying, and just kept on walking away. I chuckled as I thought to myself, "Hey guys, aren't we supposed to stop and question any strangers we might encounter in the hall—strangers who aren't wearing visitor passes?"

**Figure 5-3** Hey guys, aren't we supposed to stop and question any strangers we might encounter in the hall—strangers who aren't wearing visitor passes?

Shortly before the performance, Mr. Ruhl had conveniently taught Charles Darwin how to use the PowerPoint slides with video clips and photographs taken in the Galapagos Islands (*something I made clear to the students as I began our session together*). Once again, the students played along and engaged in make-believe as they sat "on the edges of their seats," politely listening and taking notes for the entire class period! Two weeks before this special lesson, I got the wild "last-minute" idea to go online and learn how to speak with a British accent. Looking back, I would probably give myself a grade of B- for that effort—not bad, but definitely not up to the quality of a professionally coached actor! You can watch "Darwin's visit" to my classroom here:

https://www.youtube.com/watch?v=LgaRs_EEoIg

When "Darwin" left the classroom at the end of "his" presentation, the class applauded—not something that normally happens at the end of a class! I was so proud of the kids. They "blew the test out of the water" at the end of that unit! They had mastered, like no classes before them had, the concepts of evolution, natural selection, and speciation. Take risks. The more you put into your teaching, the more you and your students will get out of it.

# CHAPTER 6

## How Transitioning from a Teacher-centered to a Student-centered Classroom Reignited My Passion for Teaching and My Students' Love for Learning

When I think back on the early years of my life as a teacher, the work was exhausting, difficult, and frustrating. I remember wondering back then if I had even made the right career choice. If it hadn't been for my stubborn streak, my earnest desire to make myself better with each passing school year, and most importantly, amazing mentors in my life, I might have burned out decades ago. Why were the first couple of years so difficult? I would distill it down to three main reasons. First of all, I was a novice when it came to classroom management and discipline. My college training more than adequately prepared me as a biologist, but no amount of "book learning" can prepare one for a classroom full of teenagers driven by raging hormones and frontal lobes that really don't develop completely until age twenty-five or so. Secondly, I didn't have files of lesson plans and activities already created and ready to go. A brand-new teacher, without any years of experience, simply hasn't had an opportunity to accumulate a "bag of tricks." Thirdly, and stemming from the first two reasons, there was the chronic mental and physical exhaustion as my evenings were filled with grading, lesson planning for the next day, and extracurricular coaching responsibilities. I was surprised, especially during that first year, to find myself working just as hard, or maybe even harder than I had in college! Now please hear me, especially pre-service teachers and new teachers! I don't mean to scare you away from pursuing this noblest of professions, but one must have a realistic view of the first two or three years of life in the classroom, count the costs, and "gird up thy loins," knowing that if you hang in there and "gut it out" in those early years, you will find yourself being rewarded with a satisfying career where you can make a real difference in the lives of students. I've alluded earlier in this book to the idea that our brains are wired for loving, and that *authentic* happiness and a sense of fulfillment result when we intentionally put decisional love into action. If there ever was a career that involved "love with its sleeves rolled up," it's teaching. So how does one survive those first two or three years, eventually paving the way to a professional life with reduced stress? First and foremost, seek out veteran colleagues who love the students and their profession, as mentors; especially those who are willing to share teaching strategies and time-tested lessons that work. Secondly, allow yourself some time to "heal" during the summer months and then spend a little time during those months "off" reflecting, writing new lessons and rewriting ones that didn't work so well. I found that investing some creative time during those summers paid off because *during* the school year, it's difficult to find time to be truly creative. I hesitate to generalize too much about this two- or three-year rule of thumb, because there are exceptions to this rule. I've seen many young teachers who do very well, even in their *first* year. I've supervised a dozen student teachers over the years and most of them excelled at the work, performed like veterans, taught me some things as well, and have turned out to be outstanding teachers.

For me, happily, somewhere during the third or fourth year, I found myself "getting the hang of it." Around the fifteen-year mark, I began experiencing that dreaded burnout. Was I getting tired of this job? Did I need a career change? Fortunately, about that time, my eyes were opened to something that I hadn't thought about much before. It wasn't so much an instantaneous revelation like Dr. Seuss' Grinch, standing on Mt. Crumpet on Christmas morning "with his feet ice cold in the snow," rather it was gradual.[1] During those first fifteen to twenty years, I had accumulated new ideas from respected colleagues, especially my friend Steve Randak, who was so willing to share ideas and activities. Steve had been my supervising teacher fifteen years earlier and was now teaching biology in a room next to mine, so we collaborated a great deal. Steve was a master at putting educational theory into practice; running a student-centered classroom based on student choice, and I couldn't help but notice how his kids responded so positively to that educational environment. Around the same time, my own children and their friends were entering their pre-teen and teenage years and this new stage in my parenting life helped me to understand even more the adolescent mind and behavior. This gradual shift in my thinking was punctuated by an exclamation mark, like a "light bulb" moment while standing in the school hallway one day during passing period between classes. As I watched the kids entering the room, it finally occurred to me, "Hey! I don't teach biology. I teach *kids* – biology." Fourteen-year-old ninth graders act immature now and then. Why? Because they *are* fourteen years old! Now I had not made an earth-shattering discovery; elementary teachers have always modeled loving kids first and the subjects they taught, second. But it was a moment of realization for me that began to make all the difference in the world. I found myself enjoying teaching and the students enjoying learning more on those days when I remembered this simple tenet: "I don't teach biology. I teach *kids* – biology." My passion for teaching seemed to be reignited when I finally took to heart the fact that there were many things more important in the lives of 14- and 15-year-olds than genes, chromosomes, cell parts, and cell division! But it was still my job to teach the students about biology, and so I found myself reinvigorated with a passion for designing teaching strategies that were nontraditional, interesting, engaging, fun, and loaded with real-world relevancy. About this same time, one day as I stood "being visible" like a sentry during lunch supervising duty, watching the kids file through the cafeteria line, it occurred to me that the kids seemed to enjoy choosing which items to put on their food trays. They liked having choices! I remember thinking, "That makes sense. Autonomy is a universal human value. So maybe incorporating student choice might work in the classroom as well." By student choice, I mean providing students with an array of learning activities within a unit that students are allowed to choose from. Allowing for student choice in this way was the key that enabled me to move from a teacher-centered classroom to a student-centered classroom. These changes that I was making were happening as the world was entering the 21st century. This was a time when the National Education Association (NEA) established that all students in the 21st century would need to learn four essential skills known as "the 4 Cs," regardless of their career paths in life: collaboration, communication, critical thinking, and creativity.[2] My first thought when I learned about the 4 Cs was, "Great. Now, in addition to all the biology content I want my students to learn, I must also teach these four essential skills as well?!" But then, to my delight, I discovered that in a student-centered environment, where I functioned more as a "guide on the side" rather than a "sage on the stage," the kids were *forced* to use these 4 Cs as they worked together in small groups on learning activities that were carefully written in a way that required higher level thinking skills and problem solving. As I watched the students working, I realized that they in fact, were practicing and therefore learning these 4 Cs as they acquired the biology content! I added two more of my own "Cs"—Choice and Caring—and my teaching philosophy became focused on these **6** Cs:

Choice (Humans love autonomy.)

Collaboration (We are wired to be social creatures.)

Communication (We are social!)

Critical Thinking (Problem solving)

Creativity (A uniquely human pleasure)

Caring (*Agape* love for the students)

And then an interesting thing happened a few years ago when I was serving on the Purdue University Biological Sciences Alumni Advisory Council (BSAAC). In one of our fall meetings, several speakers who represented Indiana businesses and industries that hire college science graduates, told us that all of the applicants for their jobs, no matter what university or college they graduated from, were well-qualified in their subject areas, however, what they were really looking for in applicants were four skills: the ability to work collaboratively with team members on projects, the ability to communicate effectively both in speaking and writing, the ability to think critically in problem solving situations, and finally, the ability to approach those problems with creativity. What they said next shocked me. They told us that only 25 percent of their applicants really demonstrated proficiency in these four essential skills! So, yes, looking back, I can see that my curriculum inclusion of NEA's four recommended essential skills: collaboration, communication, critical thinking, and creativity, along with my decision to incorporate the two additional Cs of choice and caring, are quintessential for preparing students for any and all of their career paths.

Now moving from a teacher-centered classroom to a student-centered classroom creates somewhat of a teacher paradox, because when the teacher moves off stage to function more as a facilitator or "guide on the side," on the surface, the teacher appears to become less important, apparently relinquishing classroom control. But in reality, the teacher becomes even more important. I discovered that in this student-centered classroom, I was freed up to sit down with small groups of students who had called me over for help, allowing me the opportunity to teach one on one, or one on two, or one on three, or one on four, depending on the size of the group. What a wonderful teacher-to-student ratio! In addition, working eye to eye and shoulder to shoulder with students in this way, I found it much easier to coach, mentor, nurture, and even inspire. Again, like most ideas in education, this is nothing new. Teachers in subjects like art, music, life and family studies (called "home economics" in the "old days"), and industrial technology (referred to as "shop class" in the "old days"), have been running projects-based, student-centered classrooms for years! I also discovered that my students *like* learning this way and I think it's because our brains are wired for learning this way. After all, our students are social creatures. Think about it. Earlier in Chapter 2, I imagined our prehistoric hominid ancestors out hunting for food. In those days, if you were antisocial enough to try to take down a woolly mammoth or mastodon by yourself, you probably would not have survived and so you would have been less likely to produce offspring, which eventually led to us! On the other hand, if you were a prehistoric human who knew how to work with other like-minded humans, to creatively solve problems like how to kill a large animal, then you probably had a better chance of surviving and producing offspring, which one day would lead to us. Several times students would tell me things like "Mr. Ruhl, I *love* biology class." When I would ask them why, they would give an answer along the lines of: "Because in here, we get to work together, and we get to pick the things we want to do." (*Remember, autonomy is a universal human value.*) Now the students, of course, didn't realize what I knew; yes, they had the freedom to choose their learning activities but within the limits of a two- to three-week unit and with all of their individual choices designed to cover the important concepts for each unit. While the students enjoyed learning in this environment, I found myself enjoying teaching even more! It was so professionally satisfying to see the kids working together, exploring, observing, testing hypotheses, puzzling through problems, applying learned concepts to new situations, analyzing data, and teaching one another! Not only were they learning biology, but they were also practicing collaboration, communication, critical thinking, and creativity! In other words, my students were probing higher and higher into those upper levels of Bloom's Taxonomy that we all learned about in our college education courses! Teaching became fun again!

So now for the "nuts and bolts" of how I moved from a teacher-centered classroom to a student-centered classroom . . .

I divided my year-long ninth grade biology course into two- to three-week units. At the very beginning of each unit, I would give the students a menu that contained a smorgasbord list of all the learning activities available in the unit. As you will see, the students were provided with numerous opportunities to pick and choose from the menu those activities that they would complete to achieve the learning objectives for the unit. Now this was a challenge for me because I had to write and/or borrow a whole array of activities for each unit, and design them in such a way that no matter what order a student chose to do the activities in, or what combination of activities a student chose to do, they would still achieve the required objectives for the unit. As you can imagine, this took a lot of preparation work on the front end, but remember, I was well into my teaching career by this time, so I had accumulated fairly extensive files of lesson plans, labs, and activities. I had several different student teachers who were quite taken by this approach and they would enthusiastically share with me how they wanted to teach this way when they got out "into the real world." I remember cautioning them and telling them something like, "You're going to be very busy in your first few years of teaching, so don't feel guilty if you have to resort, now and then, to more traditional, familiar teaching methods. Building a program like this takes time. Please be patient with yourself!" Since I remember what it was like to begin my first year of teaching with an empty filing cabinet, I was always happy to give my student teachers copies of all my "stuff" in an effort to give them a "head start" after they left my classroom.

In Figure 6-1 below, I've included an example menu that happens to be for the Cell Biology unit.

# Unit "Menu"

Unit **Cell Biology**          Name _____

| Activity | Points Possible | Points Earned |
|---|---|---|
| 1. *Cell Structure & Function* Study Guide (C) | 10 | _____ |
| 2. *Cell Membrane* Study Guide (C) | 10 | _____ |
| 3. *Cell Chemistry* Study Guide (C) | 10 | _____ |
| 4. How are Plant and Animal Cells Alike? (L) | 10 | _____ |
| 5. Amazing Cells (I) | 5 | _____ |
| 6. Cells Alive (I) | 5 | _____ |
| 7. Create a Cell (WB) | 5 | _____ |
| 8. The Cell Game (L) | 5 | _____ |
| 9. Immortal Life of Henrietta Lacks (WS) | 5 | _____ |
| 10. Cell Membrane and Osmosis (L) | 5 | _____ |
| 11. Building Models of Molecules (L) | 10 | _____ |
| 12. Yikes! Yeast!! (L) | 10 | _____ |
| 13. Some Cells of the Immune System (C) | 3 | _____ |
| 14. How the Cell Works (WS) | 5 | _____ |
| 15. Cells (V) | 5 | _____ |
| 16. Germs (V) | 5 | _____ |
| 17. Respiration (V) | 5 | _____ |
| 18. Understanding Viruses (V) | 5 | _____ |
| 19. The Cell – How it Works (V) | 5 | _____ |

**Figure 6-1** Example Unit Menu Continued

| | | |
|---|---|---|
| Pgs. 190-194; q. 1-5 (iPad pgs. 338-346; q. 6-10) | 3 | _____ |
| Pgs. 196-205; q. 1-5 (iPad pgs. 350-364; q. 6-10) | 3 | _____ |
| Pgs. 208-213; q. 1-4 (iPad pgs. 366-374; q. 6-9) | 3 | _____ |
| Pgs. 214-217; q. 1-3 (iPad pgs. 375-380; q. 6-8) | 3 | _____ |
| 20. 7.2 (WS) | 3 | _____ |
| 21. Reflection Sheet | 2 | _____ |
| 22. Arts & Entertainment | 10 | _____ |
| Binder | 5 | _____ |
| TEST | 25 | _____ |

On the first day of every unit, I handed out and briefly went over the list of activities on the unit with the students, before turning them loose to go to work. This system was new to the students because most of them had gotten used to learning in a traditional, teacher-centered environment. But I found that by the end of the first unit of the school year, most of the students had caught on and knew how to navigate the course, and began to realize that they were responsible for their own learning. They learned that when they came into the classroom on any particular day, they had to have a plan. They had to know what activities they were going to work on in that class period. They knew that when they entered the room, the goal for the class period was to fill up their imaginary bucket with as many points as they could because they knew their grade was based on accumulated points, not a percentage. They knew that when they finished an activity, they were required to hand it in to me. They knew I would grade it that day or that night, because they knew that on any given day when they came into class, they could check their running point total to see the progress that they were making. They knew that by the end of the two- to three-week unit, if they had accumulated sixty points, their grade for the unit would be a 'D.' Seventy points would earn them a 'C,' eighty points a 'B,' and ninety points an 'A.' They also knew they had lots of choices because if you total up all the possible points on the menu, you'll find one hundred and eighty points' worth of activities; more than any 'A' student would ever have time to do. They knew that when I graded an activity, for example, the first item on the menu entitled "Cell Structure & Function Study Guide," it would be carefully graded and they might earn ten, nine, eight, seven, or six points, etc., on the activity. Finally, they knew how many class days we would devote to working on these menu items.

Now if you've supervised young children going through a buffet line in a smorgasbord restaurant, you've probably made a few menu items required, that is: "You must put something green on your plate." In like manner, every menu in my class contained a few items that were required. One of the required activities was known as a study guide, and each unit menu had at least one study guide. You'll notice on the menu in Figure 6-1 that this unit, a particularly long unit, had three study guides listed as items 1, 2, and 3. Those study guides are basically note-taking guides that are graded. They then serve as the content material that the students will need to prepare for the twenty-five-point test that will be given on the last day of the unit. You'll find the test—another required activity—listed at the very end of the menu. The binder or notebook, the next-to-the-last item listed, is also a required activity in every unit. I would always collect their binders at the end of each unit and grade them, making sure that they were keeping and organizing all their papers for the unit, complete with table of contents, in the manner that I had prescribed for them at the beginning of the school year. All the other items on the menu (besides study guides, binder, and the test) were "up for grabs," that is, available for the choosing.

You'll notice a capital letter 'C' in parentheses after each of the listed study guides. That indicates that each of those study guides (*written by me*) are to be filled out by working through a self-paced, interactive computer tutorial that I or Steve Randak had developed during our "off times" during the summer months. Developing these computer tutorials using a powerful authoring program called Adobe Director, was sort of a creative hobby for me (*I'm a bit "geeky" that way!*). These computer tutorials were designed to take the place of the topics that I used to lecture on. Yes, developing the teacher-made software was work, but I had fun creating self-paced programs that contained text, audio, graphics, animations, video clips, interdisciplinary real-world relevancy, and humor. Steve and I wrote the tutorials so that they contained a high level of interactivity as students were frequently required to respond to understanding checks during the lessons. If a student input an incorrect response, they would see a video clip pop up on the screen giving them feedback on their answer. After an incorrect response, they would be rerouted to a short remedial lesson in the program and then required to respond correctly to the question before being allowed to move on. The highest level of interactivity involved virtual labs on the computer, where students could click and drag objects around on the screen, performing simulations of labs that are not practical in a high school setting. (*For example, in the genetics unit, the students were able to do an amniocentesis procedure on screen, culture the fetal cells in the medical lab, and perform a karyotype analysis to check the fetal chromosomes for abnormalities.*) As the students worked through the computer tutorials, they filled out their study guides, recording their notes. Students took a much more active role in their learning in this way, as opposed to sitting through a traditional whole class lecture. I managed to acquire ten Mac computers that I had spaced throughout the perimeter of my classroom (See Figure 6-2 below.), with two sets of headphones hooked up to each computer so that students could work either individually or in pairs.

**Figure 6-2** Students Working on Computer Tutorials

We are forever indebted to our school's brilliant computer tech, Brian Martin. He kept our computers up and running and up-to-date. Almost all the kids enjoyed the computer tutorials, as they were able to work at their own pace. Although I'll never forget one little boy who told me, "You know, Mr. Ruhl, I think I like your lectures better than the computer tutorials." I was a little surprised by his feedback and when I asked him why, he said, "Because when you're listening to a lecture, you only kind of half-way have to pay attention, but when you're working through the computer tutorial, you like *totally* have to pay attention." (*This still makes me chuckle when I think about it!*) Not all teachers are into developing their own computer tutorials, and I have had colleagues adapt this system to their own unique style of teaching—colleagues who are excellent, dynamic lecturers, who would lecture for a couple days on the front end of a unit while the students filled out their study guides. Then, once the lecture days were completed, they would turn the students loose to work on the menu items that were available for choice.

A visitor to my class on a typical day would have likely found some students on the computers working through the tutorials or working on a website activity. Some students would have been seen with headphones in a corner of the room, watching a short video related to the unit while writing out answers to questions that accompany the video. Some students would have been seen carrying out laboratory investigations. Some students would have been sitting around an educational game board. A few students would likely have been found at the light stand, aquariums, or incubator, tending to their ongoing science fair projects. A few students might have been seen organizing their course binders or thinking and writing reflection sheets designed for them to reflect on their learning, and self-evaluate their efforts. Many of the activities in each unit could be done in small, self-selected groups of two to five students and you would have seen me moving throughout the classroom as a facilitator. The students loved this system more than I thought they would! Several times, I would overhear some kid say to another either in the classroom or in the hallway after class something like, "I love biology, because we get to do stuff in there!" I hope you're getting an idea of why my fire for teaching was relit when I finally transitioned from a teacher-centered to a student-centered classroom based on student choice.

**Figure 6-3** The students loved this system more than I thought they would!

The rest of the items that I'll refer to in this example menu are "up for grabs," that is available for choice. Item number 4—"How are Plant and Animal Cells Alike?" is a lab activity. (*The letter 'L' in parentheses after the item means that it is a lab activity.*) This is a lab activity in which the students compare different types of plant and animal cells (*including their own cells scraped with a toothpick from the inside lining of their mouth*) under the microscope. I discovered early on, that the students were drawn to high point value items, and since I believed this was an especially important activity that I wanted them all to do, I made it worth ten points. Each activity on the menu had an accompanying handout that contained both the instructions for how to do the activity along with follow-up questions that the students were required to write out the answers to. They would then hand it in immediately upon finishing the activity. If you look at items 5 and 6 on the menu, you'll notice the letter 'I' in parentheses. This indicates that those are internet activities. I would scour the internet for high quality, interactive websites that taught concepts that I was trying to teach in the unit. I would work through these websites as a student would, composing worksheets that the students would have to fill out as they worked through the website activities. As we move on down the menu, we encounter item number 7 – "Create a Cell," a type of hands-on, minds-on activity. WB stands for White Board (*dry erase board*). In this particular unit, I had a box on the front desk that contained laminated pictures of cell parts, laminated blocks of text that contained the descriptions of the functions of the cell parts, along with little laminated names of cell parts (*Thanks for that idea, student-teacher Beth Walker!*). I had attached a piece of magnetic tape to the back of each of these laminated components so that they would stick to the white board. In this activity, if the learning station was open, one, two, or three students could take the objects in the box and construct a cell on the white board, with the blocks of text describing the functions placed next to the correct cell parts, along with the appropriate name labels. When a group had completed constructing the cell, they would call me over, and I would then check out their cell and give them an oral quiz, initial their paper, and then have them proceed to answer some written questions on their paper before handing it in. This kind of activity also showed up in my ecology unit, where the students were asked to construct a food web on the board and identify the various trophic levels. I could envision this kind of white board activity in other subject areas as well. For example, history students could be asked to construct on the white board a timeline, or to place in order the series of events connected to an important period in history. Item number 8 – The Cell Game, is a board game for three to five players with an accompanying worksheet that the students must fill out during or after playing the game. I made sure to include some questions in the worksheet that could only be answered by having completed the game. I tried to include a board game activity in each unit that would teach about some concept in the unit. A few of the board games are ones that I designed and created myself, and I sell these on an online marketplace for buying and selling teaching materials called Teachers Pay Teachers (teacherspay-teachers.com).

**Figure 6-4** I tried to include a board game activity in each unit that would teach about some concept in the unit.

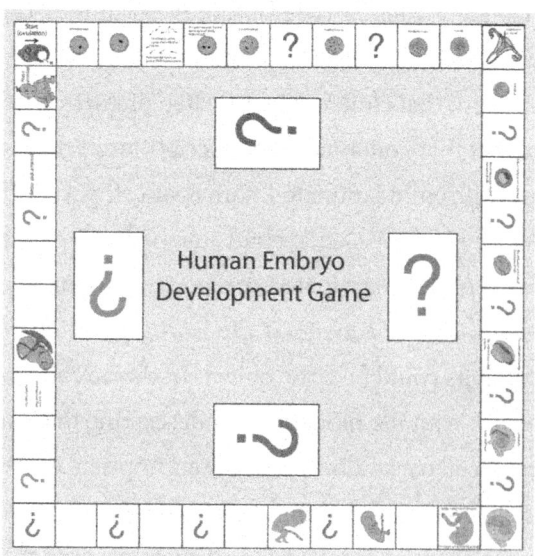

Item number 9 – Immortal Life of Henrietta Lacks (WS) is a worksheet. In this more traditional pencil and paper activity, the students are required to read an article and write the answers to questions that accompany the article. Items 10 through 12 are more lab activities that the students can choose from. Item number 13 – Some Cells of the Immune System, is another computer tutorial that I developed, although this one was not required, but available for choice. Item number 14 – How the Cell Works, is a worksheet involving the use of colored pencils. Items 15 through 19 are twenty-five-minute videos ('V' *in parentheses is for video*). I had a television monitor set up in a corner of the room with a DVD player hooked up to it along with a headphone amp with five sets of headphones. Up to five students could gather around this setup (*I even had an identical setup to accommodate another five students in the opposite corner of the room.*) with the video.

**Figure 6-5** Video work station

Following item number 19 on the menu is a list of four textbook readings with questions to answer; the most traditional of assignments. For example, the first one in the list simply means, read pages 190–194 in the textbook, write out the answers to questions 1–5 found on Page 194, and then hand that paper in. Item number 20, listed as 7.2, is another work-sheet. Item number 21 – Reflection Sheet, seemed to be a popular choice among the students, even though it was only worth two points. Its popularity was probably due to the fact that for the most part, the responses that the student was required to record on the Reflection Sheet were primarily open-ended and based on their opinions rather than black or white, right or wrong answers. Students were allowed to do one Reflection Sheet per unit and this activity was designed to get the students to thoughtfully reflect on their own learning, connect new knowledge to old knowledge, and self-evaluate their efforts. As shown in Figure 6-6 below, the student was required to choose one activity that they had already done, write down the title of the activity, a summary paragraph of the activity, a new question that they then had as a result of doing the activity, and then form a connection, that is, explain how one thing they learned about was like something that they already knew about.

**Figure 6-6** Reflection Sheet

**LEARNING ACTIVITY REFLECTION SHEET**

Name_____

Title of Activity:

Summary **Paragraph** of the Activity (must be at least 5 sentences):

New Question that *YOU* Have as a Result of Doing the Activity:

Connection (Explain how one concept that you learned about in this activity is **LIKE** something else that you already knew about.):

For example, a student might write, "All the parts of a cell are like different parts of a city because they all do different jobs." On the back side of the Reflection Sheet (See Figure 6-7 below.), there is a place for the student to evaluate their efforts in the unit.

**Figure 6-7** Self-evaluation Sheet

**SELF EVALUATION SHEET**

Name _____ Unit _____ Date _____

Think about your work during the last and current unit. Read the statements below and check the category that best describes your performance.

| | Always | Most of the Time | Some of the Time | Never |
|---|---|---|---|---|
| 1. I contribute in group work. | | | | |
| 2. I put forth the effort to reach my goal. | | | | |
| 3. I am on task the entire period. | | | | |
| 4. I ask questions when I need help. | | | | |
| 5. I give up easily. | | | | |
| 6. I come to class prepared daily. | | | | |
| 7. I work carefully and thoughtfully. | | | | |
| 8. I study for unit tests. | | | | |
| 9. I keep track of my progress. | | | | |

Item number 22 – Arts & Entertainment, was a very popular choice in every unit. Students could do this activity individually or in small groups. If they chose to do an Arts & Entertainment project, they could pick any topic they had learned about in the unit, and outside of class time, at home, produce a project that they would present to the class towards the end of the unit on the day before the test day. Their requirements for this activity were: it had to be nontraditional and creative, it had to teach some concept learned about in the unit, and the presentation itself was limited to five minutes. If you look at Figure 6-8 below, you can see a list of suggested project ideas that were made available to the students.

**Figure 6-8** Arts and Entertainment Suggestions

## ARTS and ENTERTAINMENT
### Suggestion List

Arts and Entertainment is a 10-point opportunity during each unit that allows students to use their talents in a nontraditional way that demonstrates understanding of a concept in the unit. Students are not limited to this suggestion list and any idea may be considered for points. If an idea is not listed below, please discuss it with the teacher before beginning the activity. Points are awarded based on quality of work and the amount of time invested in the activity. **Arts and Entertainment projects are to be worked on outside of class time and they will be presented near the end of the unit, the day before the test day. A student's Arts and Entertainment presentation will be limited to 5 minutes or less.**

Students may demonstrate their understanding of a concept in the unit by:

producing a video

writing and reading a poem (original- authored by the student)

writing and reading a short story (original- authored by the student)

performing a dance

writing and performing a skit

making a model

preparing a poster

reading and preparing a summary of a current science event related to the unit

designing a lab activity

designing a game

producing a comic strip

playing a musical instrument

I remember one year when a few girls who were on the dance team choreographed and performed a dance of the chromosomes during cell division! Another girl (*who ended up pursuing a professional music career*) wrote a song about DNA replication and with her guitar, performed this song, which turned out to be a great review for the rest of the class. In Figure 6-9 below, you can see an awesome example of an Arts & Entertainment project that involved a couple students building a model of a chlorophyll molecule, using colored gumdrops to represent the atoms in the molecule and toothpicks to represent the bonds holding the atoms together.

**Figure 6-9** Chlorophyll Molecule

As you can see in the photograph, chlorophyll—the pigment in green plants that enables them to absorb sunlight—is a large, complex molecule that required those two students to put in a great deal of time and thought! I guarantee they will never forget that every hydrogen atom has one bond, every oxygen atom has two bonds, every nitrogen atom has three, and every carbon atom has four. They probably worked harder on this activity than they would have if I had assigned it, because this was their own idea. I remember a talented boy, active in school plays, who produced a video in which he dressed up as two different people—Aristotle and Galileo—involved in a debate on the nature of science. I think that the reason Arts & Entertainment was a popular choice with the kids, was because it allowed them to be creative, and creativity is a uniquely human, pleasurable, self-satisfying activity. I believe that the human brain is wired for creativity and that's why the kids enjoyed it so much. As seen in Figure 6-10 below, I would imagine that our prehistoric ancestors even had smiles on their faces when they creatively told stories around the campfire about the adventures of the day's hunt.

**Figure 6-10** Creative Storytelling

The wonderful thing about creativity is that it requires critical thinking! I love this quote from Albert Einstein. If anyone understood creativity and critical thinking, it was Einstein, and he was a lot smarter than I am!

"It is the supreme art of the teacher to awaken joy in creative expression and knowledge." —Albert Einstein

By the way, as you can see in the photograph in Figure 6-11 below, one of the proudest moments in my professional life was running into Albert Einstein. It happened to be at Madame Tussauds Wax Museum in London back in 2004!

**Figure 6-11** With Albert Einstein!

As I mentioned already, the test, on the last day of the unit, covers the material in the computer tutorial study guide notes. All the non-required items on the menu that are available for choice involve the students either in the review or application of concepts learned in the study guides. As you probably have sensed from me in this chapter, moving from a teacher-centered to a student-centered classroom turned out to be a real educational "shot in the arm" for both the students and *me*, creating so many memories of serendipitous moments of joy! I remember when a team of administrators and teachers from another school system visited to observe my classes to find out more about this type of classroom set-up. They were amazed that "100 percent of these freshmen were on task 100 percent of the time in three consecutive ninety-two-minute periods!" Honestly, I don't attribute that to me. I attribute it to the system; to the methodology. How rewarding it was for me to see those ninth graders learn to take charge of their own learning, set goals, assign themselves homework, monitor their own progress, and teach one another. In the early years when I first started teaching this way, before it caught on, an assistant principal who was near retirement and "old-school"-minded, was assigned to observe and evaluate me. He stopped by for a required, scheduled observation. (*It's interesting, I always thought it would make more sense to stop in and observe unannounced, but then again, I didn't make up the rules.*) When he peeked in and saw the kids working so diligently, with me moving from group to group, he looked a little surprised and politely said, "That's okay. I'll come back on a day when you're teaching." I must say, I did get a chuckle out of that one!

Sometimes we would break from the routine and I would lecture a little bit. The twenty-minute lectures usually happened at the beginning of a class if the previous night's grading revealed some common errors or misunderstandings that most of the students were having. Those teacher-centered times looked much more traditional, and were easier for some administrators to observe and evaluate. Most importantly, they helped clear up problems that the kids were having with concepts that were more difficult to grasp.

In summary, it was a thrill for me to see the students actively engaging in these five Cs:

Choice (Humans love autonomy.)

Collaboration (We're wired to be social creatures.)

Communication (We're social!)

Critical Thinking (Problem solving)

Creativity (A uniquely human pleasure)

But don't forget our sixth C—CARING. Remember that one from Chapter 2? CARING! It's probably the most important of these Cs, because if the students perceive that their teacher genuinely cares about them as individuals, that seems to motivate them more than anything else. That makes sense, because *"the greatest of these is love. . ."*[3]

# CHAPTER 7

# "May We Live in Interesting Times."

An eight-hour, seven-part television series entitled *Evolution,* co-produced by the WGBH Educational Foundation of Boston/NOVA Science Unit and Clear Blue Sky Productions, Inc., premiered on PBS in the fall of 2001.[1] This stellar, educational series could serve as the basis for an entire comprehensive course on evolution. It's hard for me to believe that it has already been over twenty years ago! Time certainly flies, so there may be younger teachers who are unfamiliar with this outstanding series. If you're a new biology teacher, I would urge you to set aside some quiet evenings (*maybe on Friday nights or in the summer when you're "off?"*), get the popcorn ready, and binge-watch those episodes. I recently found out that the entire box set of the DVDs can be purchased on Amazon.com, and of course, the videos are on YouTube as well. The final episode of that series, entitled "What About God?" has a special place in my heart because a third of that one-hour episode was filmed at my school, Jefferson High School in Lafayette, Indiana, and in our school board meeting room just down the street! During that stressful time, my friend and colleague Steve Randak lamented, "May we live in interesting times," because of the time and emotional energy that we were forced to divert into a school-wide controversy that took our school by storm as we moved from the 20th to the 21st century. This was a time when I was serving a fifteen-year "tour of duty" as the head of the science department. We had sixteen teachers in our department, covering earth science, biology, chemistry, and physics classes, as well as a rich offering of upper-level electives in which the older students could pursue the sciences even further. Seven of us in the department were teaching some ninth grade biology classes. I myself was teaching biology, a junior/senior level Human Genetics course, and a junior/senior level Science Research Projects course in which I had the students working in various research labs across the Wabash River at nearby Purdue University. (*In Chapter 10, I have included detailed plans for any high school science teacher, who might be interested in setting up a similar course.*)

The storm began brewing when a group of students circulated a petition in which they demanded that "special creation" be added to the biology curriculum. More than half of the students in the school and even a fourth of the teachers signed it (*sigh*)! The students who led this effort were strong honors students from Christian homes, who happened to be class leaders. My sense is that they were spurred on by adults in their lives whom they highly respected. One of the chemistry teachers in our department was a Young Earth Creationist, who freely shared his viewpoints in his chemistry classes. Three of our biology teachers were teaching a special Team-Taught Biology course that the honors freshmen were placed into. These three— Steve Randak, Clare McKinney, and Amy Heath—were outstanding teachers and friends of mine that I greatly admire and collaborated with. Since the students leading this crusade were honors students, they had come from the Team-Taught Biology program. As a result, Steve, Clare, and Amy found themselves at the epicenter of a controversy that would put our school in the national spotlight. And I, as the department head, became the reluctant point-person in this time-sapping, emotional, energy-sucking, side-show. Don't get me wrong, the creation/evolution "issue" is an important topic and I believe it's critical to help students sort out their thoughts and feelings as some of them do struggle with the "issue." But, as someone who is trying to live the Christian life, and as a biologist, I find the whole controversy to be so unnecessary and unfortunate. Unfortunate because

I've seen so many young people lose their faith because well-meaning but uninformed religious adults in their lives have convinced them that science and religion are at odds, or that "the idea of evolution is from the devil." Then when these kids begin to learn science, discovering for themselves the bad science in Creationism, they conflate the young earth creationist views with Christianity and leave the church. On the other hand, I've seen science-minded kids, who have not been brought up with any kind of religious training, refuse to even a consider a life of faith, because they erroneously believe that Creationism equals Christianity. For most of my life, I've believed that the more one studies *both* science and religion with an open mind, the more one will realize that there really isn't a conflict between the two. Science deals with questions that religion doesn't and can't deal with, and religion deals with questions that science doesn't and can't deal with. They are different epistemologies or ways of knowing. If we look carefully at the opening chapters of the biblical book of Genesis, specifically the creation stories in Chapters 1 and 2, they appear, with a casual reading, to contradict modern science. But if we dig deeper, look at the audience it was written to, the pre-scientific time and culture in which it was written, the genre of the writing (*Genesis 1 is a poem!*), and the purpose of the writing, then the conflict dissolves away. John Walton, the famous Old Testament scholar and professor at Wheaton College writes in his book, *The Lost World of Genesis One*, "The Old Testament *does* communicate to us and it was written for us, and for all humankind. But it was not written *to* us. It was written to Israel."[2] You can find a short video of Professor Walton elaborating on this on the Biologos.org website, specifically at https://biologos.org/resources/understanding-genesis-with-john-walton, where he explains, "We have to approach Genesis 1 for what it is. It's an ancient document. It's not a document that was written to us. We believe the Bible was written for us, that it's for everyone of all times and places because it's God's Word. But it wasn't written to us. It wasn't written in our language; it wasn't written with our culture in mind or our culture in view."[3]

To kick-off the crusade, the leader of the student group, having been emboldened by the survey results, scheduled a meeting with me one day after school. He had never been in any of my classes, but he came to me first to plead the group's case, since I was the department head. I love to see kids become passionate about a cause, but in this case, I, of course, believed it was misguided. I know what the young man must have been thinking. "Surely Mr. Ruhl, a church elder, would be sympathetic to our cause." I, of course, listened patiently as he pled the group's case and laid out their plans and desire for the science department to revise the biology curriculum to include creationism, specifically Intelligent Design Creationism, in biology lessons whenever evolution was taught. This was a few years before the Kitzmiller v. Dover Area School District case, in which Intelligent Design Creationism was struck down by the court as not being science and therefore could not and should not be taught in science classes.[4] Brown University biology professor Kenneth Miller testified in that trial as an expert witness, providing several excellent examples showing that Intelligent Design Creationism, just like Young Earth Creationism, is not science. I highly recommend his book, *Finding Darwin's God – A Scientist's Search for Common Ground Between God and Evolution*, to anyone teaching or planning to teach biology.[5] I later met Ken Miller when he and I were speakers on a panel discussing "Classroom Conflict – Teaching the Origins of Human Beings" as part of the 2004–2005 Butler University public evening seminars on religion and science in Indianapolis. Ken was the university biology professor representative on the panel and I was the high school biology teacher representative. A humble man, Ken was a bit surprised when I asked him to autograph my copy of his book at a convention of the National Association of Biology Teachers.

During my meeting with the student ringleader, I gently explained the obvious (*at least I thought they were obvious*) legal reasons why religious viewpoints had no place in a public school classroom, and why, for reasons of scientific integrity, they had no place in a science classroom. I tried my best, within the time limits of a mere half-hour, to explain how science and religion were not enemies but different ways of knowing, and how forcing a 21st century view of science on the Genesis creation stories was in reality, not fair to the text, and *not* respecting or revering the text. I tried to explain how science is limited to exploring the natural realm and how the conclusions of evolutionary science are *neutral* to the question of the existence of God or of his involvement in creation. But that young man was on a mission. Even though I complimented him on his passion and his leadership ability, he was not convinced and I know that he was disappointed that I did not sympathize with or support his cause. So, the group caught the attention of the local newspaper, even national news (*yes—that's me you hear groaning*), and made plans to approach the school board with their proposal. I am thankful that during most of my years at Jefferson High School from 1984 through 2020, we were blessed with excellent, professional, supportive school boards and school administrators, so I knew (*or at least I hoped!*) how our school board and wise, outstanding superintendent, Dr. Ed Eiler, would respond to the kids' proposal.

As things started to heat up in the Lafayette community, Steve Randak contacted Eugenie Scott at the National Center for Science Education (*check out: ncse.ngo*). Eugenie told Steve that apparently, this was the first time in the United States that students had taken up the initiative to push for the teaching of religious explanations in science classes. That same week, before the famous packed house school board meeting, Dr. Eiler contacted me since I was the department head and a biology teacher, to set up a time when I could meet with him and one of the school board members, who he felt might have a "soft heart" for the kids and who might be sympathetic to their cause. I met with them for a couple hours one day after school, and I brought a stack of reading material for Dr. Eiler. I learned later that that brilliant man, loved and respected by the faculty, consumed those articles. Probably the most important item in the stack was one I had run across and had used as a reference for myself in my own classes. It was written by Eugenie Scott and you can find the updated article at https://ncse.ngo/creationevolution-continuum, within the National Center for Science Education's website (*ncse.ngo*).[6] The article describes all the various viewpoints regarding creation and evolution that people hold on the continuum of beliefs from the most dogmatic creation position at one end of the continuum to the most dogmatic evolution position at the other end of the continuum. It is entirely appropriate to present this continuum in class, briefly describing each of the viewpoints on the continuum. It is not appropriate, of course, for the teacher to point out the superiority of any one viewpoint. I have used a discussion of the continuum in my classes, and I have found students to be very surprised to learn that the issue is not a dichotomy with creationists on one side and evolutionists on the other. Instead, it's a continuum with a range of viewpoints that range from Flat Earthism, to Geocentrism, to Young Earth Creationism, to various forms of Old Earth Creationism such as Gap Creationism, Day-Age Creationism, Progressive Creationism, Intelligent Design Creationism, followed by Theistic Evolution, and Atheistic Evolution.

**Figure 7-1** The Creation/Evolution Continuum

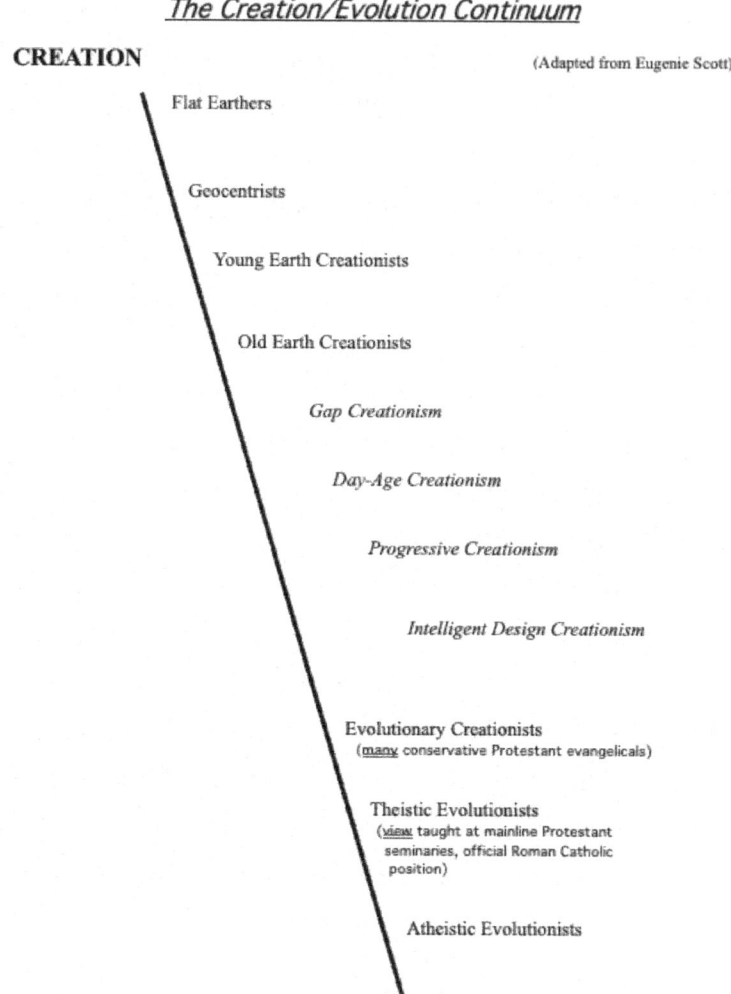

## The Creation/Evolution Continuum

**CREATION**                                   (Adapted from Eugenie Scott)

Flat Earthers

Geocentrists

Young Earth Creationists

Old Earth Creationists

*Gap Creationism*

*Day-Age Creationism*

*Progressive Creationism*

*Intelligent Design Creationism*

Evolutionary Creationists
(many conservative Protestant evangelicals)

Theistic Evolutionists
(view taught at mainline Protestant
seminaries, official Roman Catholic
position)

Atheistic Evolutionists

**EVOLUTION**

By the looks on the faces of students who I knew were struggling with how to reconcile their young, developing faith with modern science, I have even seen the "wheels turning" and heard audible sighs of relief when they discovered through this process—the realization that "Hey! I don't have to choose!" I've seen those kids then shed their fear and resistance to learning about evolution. I've included in Chapter 8, an activity sheet that

I made available for my students as a choice on the menu in my evolution unit. It is entitled "Questions about the Creation/Evolution Continuum." In that meeting with Dr. Eiler and the school board member he had invited, I went through the parts of the continuum with them. I was amazed to see the same relieved response in the school board member that I had seen in my concerned students! She was so enthusiastic about the eye-opening revelation of the continuum and she told me, "This should really be shared with the students!" At that point, if I remember right, I just smiled and agreed, "Yes, that would be a good thing to do." (*Thank you, Eugenie Scott!*)

Since we had made national news, a film crew from Clear Blue Sky Productions, Inc. came to our school during the week leading up to the school board meeting. We learned that we would be part of a documentary series on evolution that would eventually appear on PBS. Steve Randak, Clare McKinney, Amy Heath, and I also learned that we were going to be interviewed and that we would appear in this documentary. Yikes! This was both dreadful and exciting! So, we all did our homework, and came to school "pumped" and ready to be "on" the day the film crew arrived. When the director of the film crew found me before first period class, she said, "Mr. Ruhl, thank you so much for your willingness to do this, but we've decided not to interview you because none of the kids in this movement came from your classes." When she turned and went back into Steve's, Clare's, and Amy's Team-Taught Biology learning center, did I experience a mix of emotions?! I was relieved, disappointed (*Oh wow! My big chance to be on TV! Ha!*), happy, and glad to be able to proceed with a fairly normal school day. If you watch Episode 7 entitled "What About God" of the PBS documentary, I know you'll be very impressed with the way that Steve, Clare, and Amy came across in those interviews. I was very proud of them! I felt bad for Steve and Clare, though, because they received some hate mail and emails from all over the country after the program aired. I was proud of how Dr. Eiler and the school board responded. The school board meeting was open to the public and the house was packed. Dr. Eiler had advised us biology teachers that it probably would not be a good idea for us to attend that school board meeting—a wise decision. In that board meeting, which lasted for three hours, the students, their supporters, and their detractors discussed the proposed changes to our science curriculum. Fortunately, the board recognized that creationist attempts to justify the biblical creation account do not belong in the science classroom, so they voted against the students' movement. In the end, the school board made the right decision, in effect, preserving the scientific integrity of our biology courses. Dr. Eiler praised the students for their curiosity and willingness to think about such deep questions of life. He is shown towards the end of the video as he spoke at the end of the school board meeting: "There are well-defined legal and scientific definitions that set out the boundaries for biological science. Creationism does not belong in the biology curriculum . . . When we make a decision like this, we do it because we believe it is our duty and that the law requires it." Afterwards when the film crew interviewed him, he said that we would not be changing the biology curriculum. And that if they wanted to address the students' intellectual curiosity, it would have to be within the setting of a humanities course.

While our school found itself in the national spotlight during that spring semester, Steve was right when he moaned during a lunchtime gathering of biology teachers, "May we live in interesting times." That quote communicates both a blessing and a curse. I suppose the curse was in the form of the time and emotional energy that we had to invest throughout that entire controversial time. But then there were blessings that came out of those trials. We were shown incredible support by the administration and the school board, the kids respectfully accepted the board's ruling, and we biology teachers grew through the trials. Because of the ordeal, we ended up expanding our classroom lessons on evolution, intentionally developing class materials designed to simultaneously teach evolution and to nip in the bud the questions/objections often raised by some creationists. To help any biology teachers who might be interested, I have included in Chapter 8, samples of some of these activities:

1. The activity sheet referred to earlier entitled "Questions about the Creation/Evolution Continuum," that accompanies Eugenie Scott's "The Creation/Evolution Continuum."

2. A worksheet that I've entitled "Video: Introduction to Evolution." This worksheet was written to accompany a teaching video entitled "Evolution: Learning and Teaching Evolution," by PBS. This video was produced by the same people who visited our school and produced the seven part eight-hour PBS Evolution documentary.

3. A worksheet entitled "Evolution: Fossils, Genes, and Mousetraps." This worksheet is one I had the kids fill out while I showed them Kenneth Miller's engaging video.

4. "The Hominid Board Game – Examining Fossil Skulls for Clues about Human Evolution." This is a fun board game I developed that teaches the students about human evolution and phylogenetic trees.

5. "Guest Speaker – Charles Darwin on Evolution and Natural Selection." This video and accompanying worksheet is a recording of Charles Darwin's visit to my classroom!

6. Three worksheets to accompany the PBS video documentary "Your Inner Fish." These three videos:

Your Inner Fish,

Your Inner Reptile, and

Your Inner Monkey

are based on Neil Shubin's book *Your Inner Fish*.[7] I have found that these activities do an excellent job of addressing the question that creationists often pose: "Are there *ANY* transitional fossils?"

7. Letter to an irate parent opposed to the teaching of evolution. **This is obviously not something to hand out to students!** But you may find parts of it useful in your own dealings with science deniers.

## Concluding personal thoughts on creation and evolution

Those days when we biology teachers and our school were embroiled in the creation and evolution controversy that made national news were quite a major battle. Even though the outcome and our school board's culminating decision was positive, occasional small episodes of "guerrilla warfare" pop up now and then that biology teachers everywhere must deal with. The only significant issue I had with a parent involved the mother of a student that I didn't even have in class. I was in my office during my prep period and I heard an angry knock on the door. I opened the door and there was a woman I did not know. She was upset about something another biology teacher had said to her daughter in class. Since I was the science department head, I guess she thought I had more authority than I really did, so she wanted to make sure I knew about it. I think I said something benign and noncommittal like "Thanks. I'll look into it." I politely introduced myself and got her name. The conversation couldn't have been more than thirty seconds long because then she abruptly turned and marched on down the hall as she shouted a firm warning to me, "And you'll be hearing from me when you teach evolution in the spring!" I decided to send her a follow-up letter and I also emailed a copy to her. You can find a copy of that letter in Chapter 8. She never did answer my letter or my email. And even though I invited her to visit our classes, especially when we were studying evolution in the spring, she never showed up. I guess the resistance to learning about evolution will not go away anytime soon. Evolution, the unifying theory of biology; the theory that ties all of biology together, the theory that makes sense of all that we see in the biological world, is not controversial in the biological sciences community, but it still is among many parents and students, who view the controversy as a dichotomy, where one must choose between either creation or evolution. I think the unfortunate reason for this is that the loudest voices on this issue come from spokespersons, who represent the two extreme opposite ends of the Creation/Evolution Continuum that Eugenie Scott has laid out. Brilliant biologists like Richard Dawkins and Jerry Coyne on the Atheistic Evolution end of the continuum are widely published authors and speakers, who do a wonderful job of explaining biological evolution, but then they often stray into tangential anti-religion editorializing and even religion-bashing.[8] I am surprised by this because science is limited to exploring the natural, physical universe, so the existence of a non-physical God, by definition, cannot be proven or disproven using the tools and techniques of science. Evolution, in all its wonder, has nothing to do with whether or not God exists. Then, on the opposite end of the continuum, we find other influential, widely published, and generously funded voices preaching (*if I may be so blunt*) outright bad science. Millions of people have paid good money to visit *The Creation Museum* in Petersburg, Kentucky, operated by the creation apologetics organization known as *Answers in Genesis*, founded by Ken Ham.[9] In this museum, they can even see state-of-the-art, animatronic people co-existing with dinosaurs. And all the while, inadequately funded science teachers across the country are desperately working to create a scientifically literate citizenry.

It's been my experience in working with kids and their parents that it's much easier to convince them of the truth, beauty, and wonder of evolution if we first cultivate a teacher-students relationship of trust (*it worked out nicely that I taught my evolution units towards the end of the school year after months of intentional relationship building. There were, of course, references to evolution scattered throughout the year-long curriculum*) and if we're sensitive to and aware of their upbringing and beliefs. At different times over the years, there have been occasions when an individual student would come in after school because they "wanted to talk to me about evolution." Usually these were kids from strong Christian homes who were in my junior/senior level Human Genetics course; kids who were interested in pursuing biology-related careers. Having seen the overwhelming evidence for evolution in our studies of the molecular genomes of humans and other organisms, I could see that they were struggling both cognitively and emotionally with how to reconcile their faith with the scientific evidence that they were discovering. I remember going through a similar faith crisis when I was a college student so it was easy for me to be empathetic. These students were not the demanding type, pursuing a crusade to change the school's biology curriculum. These were polite, respectful kids, who were honestly searching. Since those individual students came in after school for these one-on-one conversations with me, I felt free to openly ask them about their faith and discuss their questions in ways that I certainly would *not* do in the religiously neutral, public school science classroom in front of a captive audience. In these meetings, I shared with them references from the moderate voices positioned between the opposite ends of The Creation/Evolution Continuum: voices like Francis Collins, author of books like *The Language of God* and *The Language of Science and Faith*; and Kenneth Miller, author of *Finding Darwin's God*.[10] I have even given some of these students copies of Collins' book *The Language of Science and Faith*. When I summarized the message conveyed by these authors—the message that acceptance of evolution is not incompatible with religious belief—it gave me a tremendous sense of joy to see in their facial expressions, their body language, and to hear in their voices the relief they felt in learning that a person of faith can indeed learn about and embrace the wonder and beauty of an evolving thirteen-billion-year-old creation. One of those students, Sarah, is now closing in on completing her Ph.D. focusing on cancer research, and she is still a faithful Christian with a now even higher view of God. As Charles Kingsley, 19th century Anglican clergyman, said, *"Are we to reverence Him less or more, if we hear that His might is greater, His wisdom deeper, than we ever dreamed? We knew of old that God was so wise that He could make all things; but, behold, He is so much wiser than even that, that He can make all things make themselves."*[11] Along with being in my Human Genetics class, Sarah was also a student in my Science Research Projects class. Her cancer research in a lab at Purdue University was so outstanding, that she was selected at the state level to advance to the International Science and Engineering Fair two years in a row—an extremely rare accomplishment! Since I retired from teaching, I've recently read an excellent, very readable book by Janet Kellogg Ray entitled *Baby*

*Dinosaurs on the Ark?*[12] Janet is a biology professor, who is also a Christian. I was so impressed by this book that if I find myself ever again in conversations with young, searching teenagers troubled with how to reconcile science with their faith, I'll be giving them a copy of this book. In fact, I would highly recommend this book to anyone considering becoming a high school biology teacher, because you'll need to be aware of the nature of and the reasons for the internal struggles that some of your students will have regarding the creation/evolution issue.

That 2000 spring semester was quite a trying time, but we were all thankful for the outcome. A more serious trial fell upon us years later. Steve Randak was ten years older than I was. He had been my supervising teacher when I was a student teacher, and over the years he had become a good friend and collaborating colleague. Just a couple years after he retired, he was diagnosed with glioblastoma (an aggressive type of brain cancer). When he was confined to a hospital bed in their house, under hospice care, I occasionally would stop by to visit with him and his wife Linda, before heading home after school. It was so difficult to watch his decline. Steve was a brilliant biologist, the most creative biology teacher I have known, one of the kindest human beings I have known, and he loved kids. I think Steve was an agnostic, but I asked him, "Steve, is it okay if I pray with you?" Wouldn't you know, he said, "Yes, please do." Dr. Eiler even came with me during one of those last meetings. Steve had been an avid reader, but eventually he got to the point where he was unable to read, so I would read to him every time I visited and he thoroughly enjoyed it, never expressing a bit of self-pity. The book we read had just come out and was entitled *Your Inner Fish: A Journey into the 3.5-Billion-Year History of the Human Body*, by Dr. Neil Shubin. We never finished that book together because Steve died at 9:40 PM on August 23, 2011. He was 66 years old.

**Figure 7-2** Steve Randak – my mentor and friend

# CHAPTER 8

# Evolution Teaching Resources

In this chapter, I'll be sharing with fellow biology teachers some teaching materials that I have developed. I've included them in this chapter, but if you are interested in using any of them in your own classes, you may download ready-to-use copies from my website:

**joeruhlteacherpdspeaker.net**

    1. **Activity Sheet - "Questions About the Creation/Evolution Continuum"** that accompanies Eugenie Scott's "The Creation/ Evolution Continuum." It is entirely appropriate (legally and pedagogically) to use this activity, *IF* the teacher doesn't force a particular viewpoint on the kids. The strength of "The Creation/Evolution" diagram and worksheet is the kids' eyes will be opened as they learn that the "issue" is not a simple dichotomy (*evolution vs. creation*), but rather, a continuum. **I would recommend that the teacher first study the article and use the information in it to build a PowerPoint presentation to illustrate each of the positions along the continuum. Then in class, briefly summarize each of the positions, starting at one end of the continuum and working towards the other end.**

**Questions About the Creation Evolution Continuum**

Using your teacher's presentation of "The Creation Evolution Continuum" and the diagram of the continuum on Page 2 of this document, write out the answers to the following questions.

1. What is a *dichotomy*?

2. What is a continuum?

3. Explain why the creation/evolution "issue" is a continuum of ideas rather than a dichotomy.

4. Explain one way that a Flat Earther would support the idea that the earth is flat.

5. How is a Geocentrist like a Flat Earther?

6. Explain one way that a Geocentrist would support the idea that the earth is the center of the universe.

7. How old is the earth according to a Young Earth Creationist?

8. Gap Creationists believe that the earth we see today was formed in six 24-hour days. How does that fit with their idea that the earth is very old (4.5 billion years old)?

9. How would a Day-Age Creationist back up their acceptance of the earth being very old (4.5 billion years old)?

10. Do Progressive Creationists accept *any* evolution? Explain.

11. Do Intelligent Design Creationists accept natural selection?

12. Intelligent Design Creationists believe that some biological structures, like DNA, are too _____ to have evolved by natural selection.

13. Would Theistic Evolutionists accept the scientific evidence for evolutionary descent with modification (that some invertebrates evolved into fish; some fish evolved into amphibians; some amphibians evolved into reptiles; some reptiles evolved into mammals; some mammals evolved into humans)?

14. Do Theistic Evolutionists believe in God?

15. Are Evolutionary Creationists and Theistic Evolutionists different from each other *scientifically*?

16. Are Evolutionary Creationists and Theistic Evolutionists different from each other *theologically*?

17. How is Atheistic Evolution like Theistic Evolution?

18. How is Atheistic Evolution different from Theistic Evolution?

## The Creation/Evolution Continuum

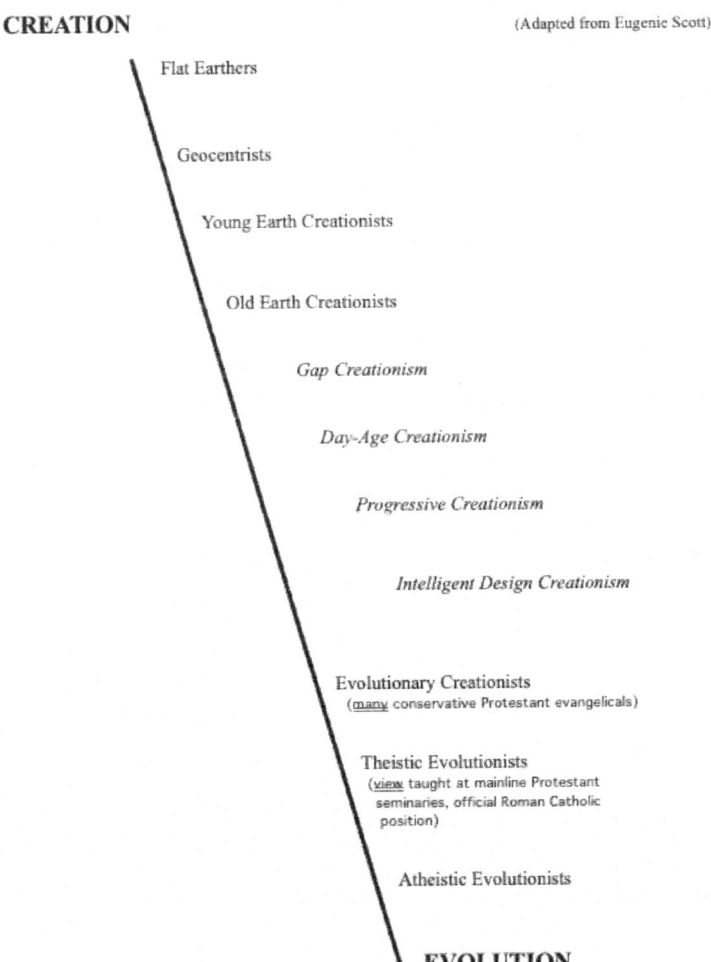

**CREATION**
(Adapted from Eugenie Scott)

Flat Earthers

Geocentrists

Young Earth Creationists

Old Earth Creationists

*Gap Creationism*

*Day-Age Creationism*

*Progressive Creationism*

*Intelligent Design Creationism*

Evolutionary Creationists
(many conservative Protestant evangelicals)

Theistic Evolutionists
(view taught at mainline Protestant
seminaries, official Roman Catholic
position)

Atheistic Evolutionists

**EVOLUTION**

2. **Worksheet - "Video: Introduction to Evolution."** This worksheet was written to accompany a teaching video entitled "Evolution: Learning and Teaching Evolution," by PBS. This video was produced by the same people who visited our school and produced the seven part eight-hour PBS Evolution documentary. I checked on Amazon.com and this video is listed as unavailable, but you can find it here:

https://www.youtube.com/watch?v=glHdXKTLgpo&list=PLo-cAByqkj4BXKFWy9pZXq0QBp6W6Pj5qg&index=2

The video is divided up into seven 6–7-minute segments. It provides an excellent introduction to evolution and I used it on the first day of the evolution unit with my students to introduce the unit.

**Video Introduction to Evolution**

As you watch this video on the "Introduction to Evolution," write out the answers to the following questions.

**Segment 1** – *Isn't Evolution Just a Theory?*

1. How does the definition of the word "theory" in science differ from the way "theory" is used in common everyday language?

2. What four things does a theory pull together in science?

a.


b.


c.


d.

3. Darwin thought that if the globe (earth) changed, then

_____ would have to change, or they would become extinct.

4. All scientific theories, including the theory of evolution, help us to

_____

_____.

**Segment 2** – *Who Was Charles Darwin?*

    5. What experience opened Darwin's eyes to the idea of evolution?

    6. What was Darwin's one "simple and elegant idea?"

    7. Why did Darwin hesitate to publish his ideas?

**Segment 3** – *How Do We Know Evolution Happens?*

    8. What is the principal evidence that life has changed through time?

    9. Basilosaurus is an intermediate or "transitional form" because it has _____.

**Segment 4** – *How Does Evolution Really Work?*

Don't worry about missing the next one if you can't keep up with the video, because the video will show each of the following points again after initially mentioning them.

    10. What are the four parts of Darwin's idea of natural selection?

        a.

        b.

        c.

        d.

    11. What controls the length of the bill in hummingbirds?

**Segment 5** – *Did Humans Evolve?*

    12. What is the difference between a relative (like a cousin) and an ancestor (like a grandparent)?

    13. How much of our DNA do we share with chimpanzees?

14. Do we share more or less DNA with rats (than we do with chimps)?

**Segment 6** – *Why Does Evolution Matter Now?*

15. Tuberculosis (TB) is caused by what?

16. Russian TB has evolved and become resistant to antibiotics. Why should we be concerned about Russian TB?

17. Why does our survival depend upon an understanding of evolution?

**Segment 7**– *Why is Evolution Controversial Anyway?*

18. Why is evolution (in the minds of some people) controversial?

19. Most Jews, Protestants, Catholics, and other religious people _____ evolution.

20. The following three Bible believers featured in this video find no conflict between science (evolution) and their religious faith:

Emi Hayashi – Wheaton College student majoring in science

Beth Stuebing – Wheaton College student majoring in science

Dr. Kenneth Miller – Brown University biologist

Why do these people believe there is no conflict between science and religious faith?

**3. Worksheet – "Evolution: Fossils, Genes, and Mousetraps."** This worksheet (originally conceived by colleague David Hunt) is one I had the kids fill out while I showed them Kenneth Miller's video that you can find here:

https://www.biointeractive.org/professional-learning/science-talks/evolution-fossils-genes-and-mousetraps

If I only had a day or two to teach about evolution, this video is what I would use.

## Evolution: Fossils, Genes, and Mousetraps

1.  Dr. Ken Miller is a biology professor at Brown University. List two books that he has written.

    a.

    b.

2.  List two states that have recently been involved in major political battles concerning the teaching of evolution.

    a.

    b.

3.  What do theories do?

4.  Why did Dr. Miller object to the Georgia School Board's sticker being placed inside the front cover of the Miller and Levine *Biology* textbook?

5.  From the video clip of *The Colbert Report*, summarize Dr. Miller's thirty-second answer to the question "What is evolution?"

6.  Evolution does not _____ one species into another, it _____ them into _____ species that go their own separate ways.

7.  Explain how recent whale fossil discoveries have cleared up doubts about "missing links."

8.  Chromosomes have _____ on their ends.

9.  Human chromosome #2 is actually two _____ _____ joined together end-to-end. We know this because human chromosome #2 has _____ __ in the middle.

10. What Pennsylvania town was involved in a 2005 federal court case involving the teaching of evolution?

11. Explain the events that led to this trial.

12. Religious people believe in an _____ design to the universe that is the work of the _____. But this is _____ what is meant by Intelligent Design (**ID**). Intelligent Design (**ID**) is the claim that "_____," supernatural intervention is _____ to account for the origins of _____.

13. Supporters of **ID** claim, "_____ cannot explain the origin of _____ cellular machines."

14. The idea of "irreducible complexity" claims that something cannot be produced by _____ because when one part is _____, the "machine" will not work.

15. A leading supporter of **ID**, Dr. Michael Behe, who testified at the Dover trial in support of **ID**, claims that "any precursor to an _____ complex system that is missing a part is by definition _____."

16. How did Dr. Miller refute Dr. Behe's idea of "irreducible complexity?"

17. Dr. Behe argued that some biochemical systems such as the flagellum and blood-clotting reactions are "irreducibly complex." ***Does the scientific evidence support this claim?***

*Circle:* **YES** or **NO**      ***EXPLAIN YOUR CHOICE***

18. Which witnesses, those *for* **OR** *against* **ID**, provided the best evidence during the trial that ID is not science, but rather a religious belief masquerading as science?

_____      ***Explain***

19. On the witness stand, Dr. Behe, a leading supporter of ID, admitted that "if you change the _____ of science so that **ID** can be considered science then _____ could be considered science and could be taught in _____ classrooms."

20. a) It is often claimed that to be "fair," **ID** must be included as a normal part of a science class. However, Dr. Miller believes that its inclusion would be "unfair." Why does Miller believe this? Use the following progression in your answer:

Novel (new) Scientific Claim

Research

Peer Review

Scientific Consensus

Classrooms & Textbooks

    b) Why is intelligent design rejected by most of the scientific community?

**Answer Key for Evolution: Fossils, Genes, and Mousetraps**

1. Dr. Ken Miller is a biology professor at Brown University. List two books that he has written.

   a. *High school Biology textbooks*

   b. *Finding Darwin's God: A Scientist's Search for Common Ground Between God and Evolution*

2. List two states that have recently been involved in major political battles concerning the teaching of evolution.

   a. *Georgia*

   b. *Kansas*

3. What do theories do?

*Theories help us make predictions about the natural world.*

4. Why did Dr. Miller object to the Georgia School Board's sticker being placed inside the front cover of the Miller and Levine *Biology* textbook?

*The sticker implied that in all of biology, only knowledge about evolution is suspect. In reality, all of science must be approached with a critical, open mind.*

5. From the video clip of *The Colbert Report*, summarize Dr. Miller's thirty-second answer to the question, "What is evolution?"

*The study of evolution shows us that all life on the planet is related and that we humans are a product of evolution.*

6. Evolution does not <u>transform</u> one species into another, it <u>splits</u> them into <u>separate</u> species that go their own separate ways.

7. Explain how recent whale fossil discoveries have cleared up doubts about "missing links."

*Over the last several years, numerous transitional fossils have been found, providing a complete picture of the evolution of modern whales from land-dwelling, wolf-like ancestors.*

8. Chromosomes have *telomeres* on their ends.

9. Human chromosome #2 is actually two *chromosomes* joined together end-to-end. We know this because human chromosome #2 has *telomeres* in the middle.

10. What Pennsylvania town was involved in a 2005 federal court case involving the teaching of evolution?

*Dover*

11. Explain the events that led to this trial.

*Some of the local school board members wanted the biology teachers to teach Intelligent Design (ID) in their biology classes. The biology teachers refused to do so.*

12. Religious people believe in an *intelligent* design to the universe that is the work of the *designer*. But this is *not* what is meant by Intelligent design (**ID**). Intelligent design (**ID**) is the claim that "*puff of smoke*," supernatural intervention is *required* to account for the origins of *living things*.

13. Supporters of **ID** claim, "*evolution* cannot explain the origin of *complex* cellular machines."

14. The idea of "irreducible complexity" claims that something cannot be produced by *evolution* because when one part is *missing*, the "machine" will not work.

15. A leading supporter of **ID**, Dr. Michael Behe, who testified at the Dover trial in support of **ID**, claims that "any precursor to an *irreducibly* complex system that is missing a part is by definition *nonfunctional*."

16. How did Dr. Miller refute Dr. Behe's idea of "irreducible complexity?"

*He used a mousetrap. He showed how the mousetrap could still function even when one or more parts are removed. He also showed how the individual parts could have different functions of their own. Another possible answer—he showed how different microbes use components of the flagellum "machine" for other purposes. He also showed how other organisms are able to clot their blood even though they are missing proteins that are part of the human blood-clotting cascade.*

17. Dr. Behe argued that some biochemical systems such as the flagellum and blood-clotting reactions are "irreducibly complex." **Does the scientific evidence support this claim?**

***Circle:* YES or NO      *EXPLAIN YOUR CHOICE***

*No. See the answer key for number 16 above.*

18. Which witnesses, those *for* **OR** *against* **ID**, provided the best evidence during the trial that ID is not science, but rather a religious belief masquerading as science?

*For*             ***Explain***

*The expert witnesses for Intelligent Design claimed that in order to include ID as a scientific theory, that the rules for doing science would have to be changed, and that supernatural events would have to be included as part of scientific inquiry. In this change in the rules for doing science, astrology could then be included as a science.*

19. On the witness stand, Dr. Behe, a leading supporter of ID, admitted that "if you change the _rules_ of science so that **ID** can be considered science then _astrology_ could be considered science and could be taught in _science_ classrooms."

20. a) It is often claimed that to be "fair," **ID** must be included as a normal part of a science class. However, Dr. Miller believes that its inclusion would be "unfair." Why does Miller believe this? Use the following progression in your answer:

Novel (new) Scientific Claim

Research

Peer Review

Scientific Consensus

Classrooms & Textbooks

*Before a novel scientific claim ends up in classroom textbooks, it must pass through several rigorous tests of acceptance by the scientific community. It must be researched to produce data. The results of that research must undergo peer review. If the finding survives peer review, then it must be accepted by the scientific community (scientific consensus). Only then will the new idea be written up and published in classroom textbooks. Miller believes that including ID in science textbooks would be unfair because the proponents of ID want to skip research, peer review, and scientific consensus, and jump all the way from novel idea to classroom textbooks.*

b) Why is intelligent design rejected by most of the scientific community?

*The evidence shows it is wrong.*

4. **Lab – "The Hominid Board Game – Examining Fossil Skulls for Clues About Human Evolution."** This is a board game I developed that you can find here:

https://www.teacherspayteachers.com/Product/Hominid-Board-Game-Examining-Fossil-Skulls-for-Clues-About-Human-Evolution-7178697

As the students play this board game, they will:

a. Locate and piece together a "fossil hominid skull."

b. Describe and collect data on their own fossil find.

c. Work together with the other members of their game group to hypothesize and construct a "family tree diagram" (phylogenetic tree) showing the relationships between the hominid skulls represented in the game.

d. Hand in their reconstructed skull, evolutionary tree, and answers to the lab questions.

5. **Worksheet – "Guest Speaker – Charles Darwin on Evolution and Natural Selection."** This video and accompanying worksheet can be found here:

https://www.teacherspayteachers.com/Product/Guest-Speaker-Charles-Darwin-on-Evolution-and-Natural-Selection-5980500

This video is a recording of Charles Darwin's visit to my classroom!

6. **Three worksheets to accompany the PBS video documentary "Your Inner Fish."** These three videos:

Your Inner Fish,

Your Inner Reptile, and

Your Inner Monkey

are based on Neil Shubin's book *Your Inner Fish*. I have found that these activities do an excellent job of addressing the question that creationists often pose: "Are there *ANY* transitional fossils?" You can purchase these videos here:

https://shop.pbs.org/WC5392.html?utm_source=PBS&utm_medi-um=Link&utm_campaign=pbs_content_yourinnerfish_buydvdto-pnav

There's also an excellent set of free classroom resources to accompany these videos that you can find here:

https://www.biointeractive.org/classroom-resources/activity-your-inner-fish

## Your Inner Fish

As you watch the video entitled "Your Inner Fish," answer the following questions.

1. Dr. Shubin said that some of the road signs to our own bodies are seen in _____.

2. Fossils show us that fish were the first creatures to have what?

3. How long ago were the first primitive fish swimming in the oceans?

4. How long ago did amphibians appear on land?

5. How long ago did mammals appear on land?

6. What is striking about the wiring of the nerves in the human head compared to the fish head?

7. What part of the human anatomy is something that we just don't see in fish?

8. Describe the pattern in limb bones (discovered by Sir Richard Owen) that we can see in the limb bones of all amphibians, reptiles, birds, and mammals.

9. How did Charles Darwin explain this similarity in all land animals?

10. What bold prediction did Darwin make when comparing fish that had fins to animals with bony limbs?

11. How was the fossil species *Ichthyostega* different from modern amphibians?

12. How was the fossil species *Ichthyostega* different from fish?

13. What were Dr. Shubin and his colleagues looking for in northern Canada?

14. What is remarkable if you compare an early human embryo to an early fish embryo?

15. What do the gill arches in a fish embryo develop into?

16. What do the gill arches in a human embryo develop into?

17. Where do the gonads first form in a fish embryo?

18. Where do the gonads first form in a human embryo?

19. Where are the gonads located in an adult fish?

20. Describe the movement or migration of the gonads as a human male embryo develops.

21. What embryo development process was Dr. Haven studying in chicken embryos?

22. Dr. Haven discovered that the gene that controls the development of the limb in the fruit fly is the same gene that controls the development of the limb in the _____.

23. What did they nickname this gene?

24. Besides fruit flies and chickens, in what other organisms does this gene control limb formation?

25. When Dr. Dahn put a bead containing this control gene on the opposite side of the limb bud of a skate embryo, what happened?

26. List three fish like features that *Tiktaalik* has.

27. What three important features did Tiktaalik have that are found in us and *not* in fish?

28. What was important about the inside of *Tiktaalik's* fins?

29. What was *Tiktaalik* able to do with its strong fins?

30. Our evolutionary history can be found not only in our bones, flesh, and muscles, but it's also found in our _____.

## Your Inner Reptile

As you watch the video entitled "Your Inner Reptile," answer the following questions.

1. What fossil did Dr. Shubin and his colleagues discover at the Bay of Fundy dig site?

2. What two classes of vertebrate animals did this fossil fish contain a mix of?

3. What two reptile structures are present in us during our embryo development?

4. a. What was the major challenge that amphibians had to face when they moved onto land?

   b. How did they get around this problem?

5. a. What was the major challenge that reptiles had, living on land?

   b. Describe two ways that reptiles got around this problem.

6. Reptiles and birds have genes that control the formation of yolk. What do reptiles and birds use their yolk sac for?

7. a. Do we humans have genes for making a yolk sac?

   b. Why doesn't the human yolk sac contain proteins for nourishing the human embryo?

8. In order to survive in the dry air on land, what did reptiles evolve to protect their bodies from drying out?

9. a. How is our skin the same as that of a reptile's?

   b. How is our skin different?

10. In the fossils found in the Karoo region of South Africa, fossils were found that contained a mix of what two different classes of vertebrate animals?

11. What mammal-like feature was found in the mouth of the fossil reptile called *Gorgonopsia*?

12. How are the teeth of *Gorgonopsia* different from usual reptile teeth?

13. The Permian mass extinction created new opportunities for those that survived, such as burrowing animals that lived underground. What do the pits on the upper jaw of fossilized *Thrinaxodons* tell us about this animal?

14. What did later mammal-like reptiles like *Tritheledontids* begin using hair for?

15. Dr. Abigail Tucker removed a tiny piece of skin from the jaw of a mouse embryo and then placed it in an incubator. What did this tiny piece of skin develop into?

16. a. What gene caused that piece of skin from the embryos' jaw to develop into a tooth?

    b. List three other skin structures that are produced by this gene.

17. a. In her work studying the embryos of tiny opossums at different stages of development, how many middle ear bones (like we see in reptiles) did she find in the earliest embryos?

    b. How many middle ear bones did she find in the latest stages of opossum embryo development?

    c. Where did the extra middle ear bones come from?

18. In China, a one hundred and ninety-five-million-year-old fossil was found called *Hadrocodium*. Describe the structure of its ear bones that led scientists to regard it as one of the earliest mammals.

19. A surprisingly large brain (compared to its body size) was found in *Hadrocodium* fossils. Why was its large brain advantageous?

20. What event opened up endless possibilities for these early, primitive mammals to gain a foothold, flourish, and evolve into all the species of mammals that we see today?

## Your Inner Monkey

As you watch the video entitled "Your Inner Monkey," answer the following questions.

1. One of the earliest primates, *Notharctus tenebrosus*, lived in what kind of environment?

2. How was its hand different from other primates?

3. What was it able to do with this new kind of hand?

4. What new change occurred in its vision?

5. Explain what happened when an OPSIN gene for color-vision was inserted into the retina of a normal red-green colorblind monkey.

6. What did this show about the monkey's brain?

7. While our hominid ancestors' color-vision improved, what did we lose as a "trade-off?"

8. a. In 1974, Dr. Donald Johanson discovered the famous hominid known as "Lucy." What part of her body was ape-like?

b. What feature of her body was more like that of a modern human?

9. *Ardipithecus ramidus* was even older than the *Australopithecus afarensis* specimen (nicknamed "Lucy"). "Ardi" shows more of a mix of traits like you would see in a transitional fossil. Besides being able to walk upright, what was she also good at?

10. What is the downside of us being able to walk upright today?

11. How did the shape of our backbone change so that we could walk upright?

12. What was the unfortunate result of that change in the shape of our backbone?

13. When our ancestors walked upright, what did it allow them to be able to do with their hands?

14. Humans and other vertebrates, even fish, have something in common when we look at their brains. What three major parts of the brain do humans and fish both have?

15. Going back before fishes, we come to a primitive worm-like creature called *Amphioxus*, that surprisingly, has a primitive nerve cord running along the length of its back (something worms do not have). If we examine the genetic make-up of *Amphioxus*, we see that it has the same _____ that contain instructions for building the spinal cord that we have.

**7. Letter to an irate parent opposed to the teaching of evolution**

**This is obviously not something to hand out to students!** But you may find parts of it useful in your own dealings with science deniers. (Look at the date when I wrote that letter. Who would have known that our world would change forever the very next day?)

September 10, 2001

Joseph D. Ruhl – Science Dept. Head

Jefferson High School

1801 S. 18th. St.

Lafayette, IN 47905

(765-772-4700, ext. 5032

jruhl@lsc.k12.in.us

Dear Mrs. _____,

Thank you for stopping in at the science department the other day. I appreciate your interest and involvement in your daughter's education. We need for more parents to be actively involved in and concerned about their children's education.

I hope your conversation with your daughter's biology teacher went well and that it was productive.

I remember you mentioned that we will be hearing from you when we teach evolution. As a Christian and a biologist, the topic of the creation/evolution "issue" has been of passionate interest to me for the last thirty years, so naturally, I was encouraged by your interest in the topic. Again, because of our desire for parents to be involved and interested in what their children are learning, please feel free to come in and observe some lessons, especially during the evolution unit.

I realize (and it breaks my heart) that some people have become polarized on the "issue." So much needless time and energy has been devoted to this "issue." Science and religion seek answers to different kinds of questions so they are not *conflicting* ways of knowing but rather, *different* ways of knowing. As such, it would be inappropriate, for example, to ask "Does God send the rain, or does rain form through a well-documented scientific process known as the water cycle?" Many people would answer "Yes!" to both parts of that question. If I may share another (personal) example. Do I believe that our two children are gifts from God; that they were "knit together in their mother's womb" as described in Psalm 139:13 (the religious or faith explanation)?[1] The answer to that question is "yes." Do I also accept the scientific explanation that a child forms when:

1. egg and sperm unite,

2. Twenty thousand plus genes (DNA molecules) within the forty-six chromosomes inside the nucleus of that fertilized egg begin the process of controlling the manufacture of RNA,

3. RNA molecules proceed to instruct the dividing cells to produce enzymes and other proteins,

4. those proteins serve as the molecular machinery of the cells,

5. different genes in different cells are selectively turned either on or off, resulting in differentiation, leading to the development of different kinds of body parts,

6. resulting, eventually, in a baby made up of trillions of exquisite, individually working cells?

My answer is "yes" to that question as well.

Indeed, to many people (scientists included), science and religion are not conflicting ways of knowing. They are complementary ways of knowing. As science teachers, we are charged, though, with teaching scientific explanations in science classes. It is so important for all concerned parties to realize that scientific explanations of natural phenomena do not negate the existence or sovereignty of God.

Thank you for your interest. Please let me know if you would like to visit any of our classes. We're excited about getting students interested in science, and we welcome the opportunity to share that excitement with others!

Sincerely,
Joseph D. Ruhl

# CHAPTER 9

# More Biology Teaching Resources

In Chapter 1, I told a story about an activity that I did with my ninth grade biology students early in the school year known simply as the pond water lab. Its official title is "Hunting for Freshwater Invertebrates." This activity was always such a big hit with the students that I've included it here in this chapter, along with a few other fun, guided-inquiry labs. Again, if you are interested in using any of them in your own classes, you can download ready-to-use copies from my website:

**joeruhlteacherpdspeaker.net**

1. **Lab – "Hunting for Freshwater Invertebrates."** You will need to have available a few copies of freshwater macroinvertebrates identification guides so the students will be able to look up the specimens they have discovered. Back in Chapter 1, you will find instructions for the teacher on how to collect pond water samples and to concentrate the organisms so that the students will be sure to find them in the lab.

### Lab —Hunting for Freshwater Invertebrates

J. Ruhl
(with thanks to Dr. C.Drewes,
Iowa State University)

## Introduction

*Invertebrates* are animals that do not have a backbone. Since we humans are **vertebrates**, we tend to pay more attention to the vertebrates of the world (humans, cats, dogs, cows, birds, etc.) **In reality, more than 95 percent of all the species of animals on this planet are invertebrates!** Invertebrates are fascinating organisms because they are so different from us in many ways, yet like us in some ways. In this lab, you will take a safari through some pond water and identify some of the freshwater invertebrates living in it. Freshwater invertebrates are important because they make up some of the initial steps in many food chains.

## Materials

1 binocular dissecting microscope with light source

1 glass Petri dish

1 plastic pipet

1 concave microscope slide

1 coverslip

a source of pond water

turkey baster

## Instructions

1. Using the turkey baster, place a small amount of pond water in a Petri dish.

2. Place this Petri dish under a binocular dissecting microscope, and scan the Petri dish for tiny freshwater invertebrates. If you find an interesting specimen that swims too fast for you to see, suck the organism up in a plastic Pipet and squirt it into a concave micro-scope slide. Place a coverslip over the specimen and then view it under the dissecting microscope.

3. Select four different kinds of invertebrates and carefully draw them in the spaces indicated on the next page.

4. Using the identification materials in the lab, identify each of the four organisms that you draw. Under each specimen drawing, label it with its name. Below is a list of some example organisms that you might find:

Hydra

Flatworms

Roundworms

Segmented worms such as *lumbriculus* (mud worms)

Segmented worms such as leeches

Clams

Bryozoans

Rotifers

Ostracods

Copepods

Scuds

Daphnia

Mites

Insect larvae or nymphs

Organism #1                    Organism #2

_____               _____

(Name)                         (Name)
Organism #3                    Organism #4

_____               _____

## 2. Lab – "Are You Stronger (gram for gram) than a Cockroach?"

I found it best to use this activity more like a demonstration because it's not easy to tie a harness made of thread around a Madagascar hissing cockroach! I had the students gather around a lab table with me as I quickly fashioned a harness, by making a slip knot in the thread, putting the loop over its head, and then pulling the loop tight so that it encircled the cockroach's body just in front of its legs. We then did the lab together as a whole class activity. Madagascar hissing cockroaches are sold in many pet stores, and it's very easy to maintain a colony of them in the classroom. Just google "How to keep Madagascar hissing cockroaches."

**Lab —Are You Stronger (gram for gram) than a Cockroach?**

## Introduction

In this lab activity, you will find out how much weight a Madagascar Hissing cockroach can pull, and then compare its strength to yours. How much weight could you pull if you were as strong (gram for gram) as a cockroach?

## Materials

1 adult hissing cockroach

paper towels

1 plastic Petri dish

sewing thread

clear tape

pennies

1 balance

## Instructions

1. Lay out and tape to the table a line of paper towels about eighteen inches long.

2. Tie a nonslip noose on the end of a piece of an eight-inch piece of thread.

3. Place the noose over the head of an adult hissing cockroach.

4. Tape the other end of the thread to the underside of a plastic Petri dish.

5. Place the cockroach on the paper towel track and see if the animal can pull the Petri dish.

6. Add a penny to the dish and see if the cockroach is still able to pull the dish.

7. Keep adding pennies (one at a time) until the cockroach is no longer able to pull the load.

8. Place the cockroach on a balance. How much does the cockroach weigh?

9. Place the Petri dish on a balance. How much does the Petri dish weigh?

10. How many pennies in the Petri dish was the cockroach able to pull?

11. What was the total mass that the cockroach was able to pull (mass of pennies plus mass of the Petri dish) **Show your work.**

12. How many times its own mass was the cockroach able to pull? **Show your work.**

13. If you were as strong as a cockroach, how much mass would you be able to pull? **Show your work.**

3. **Lab – "Flower Dissection Lab".** Modern biology state standards don't cover plant anatomy, but as biologists, we understand the importance of plants in our lives and it's vital that our students understand that flowering plants provide us with things that would be tough to live without; things like oxygen, building materials for our homes, and food. Because plants are the MVPs in any ecosystem, I added this lab activity to my ecology unit as one of the choices on the "smorgasbord" menu. I was amazed to learn that basic flower anatomy was completely unknown to my ninth

graders, and they loved the activity! They were surprised to learn about the sex lives of flowering plants!

The best source for fresh flowers in this activity is your local florist shop. Just ask for lilies, which they are usually able to get anytime of the year. Because of the relatively large size of lilies, the structures will be easy for the students to find.

## Lab —Flower Dissection Lab

### Introduction

Flowering plants are the most recently evolved members of the plant kingdom. Many of the plants that we are most familiar with belong to this group. Plants such as hardwood trees, corn, soybeans, grass, clover, roses, daisies, and daffodils produce flowers that are actually the reproductive organs of these plants. The purpose of this lab is to dissect a flower specimen to learn about the reproductive structures found in it and how they function.

### Materials

1 dissecting microscope

1 compound microscope

1 microscope slide

1 cover slip

1 forceps (tweezers)

1 single edged razor blade or scalpel

1 flower specimen

your textbook

### Instructions

1. Using the index of your textbook as a reference, locate the section that contains a diagram of the parts of a flower with descriptions of their functions.

2. Again, using your textbook as a reference, list four characteristics of plants that are known as **monocots**.

    a.

    b.

    c.

    d.

3. List four characteristics of plants that are known as **dicots**.

    a.

    b.

    c.

    d.

4. Is your flower specimen from a monocot or a dicot plant?

    How do you know?

5. Examine the diagram of the parts of a flower in your textbook. How many petals does your flower specimen have?

    What color are they?

    Many flowers depend upon pollinators and the pollinators in turn, depend upon the flowers. What function do these flower petals play in the flower-pollinator relationship?

6. What three structures make up the pistil or female part?

    a.

    b.

    c.

7. What two structures make up the stamens or male part?

    a.

    b.

8. What color is the pistil in your specimen?

9. What color are the anthers in your specimen?

10. How many anthers are there in your flower?

11. What do the anthers produce?

12. What special cells are made inside the ovary?

13. Carefully use the forceps to remove the pistil.

Using a single-edged razor blade or scalpel, carefully slice the ovary open (lengthwise).

Examine the contents of the ovary under the dissecting microscope.

What do you see inside the ovary?

How many are there?

14. Using the forceps, carefully remove one of the stamens.

Scrape some of the pollen grains from the anther onto a microscope slide.

Place a coverslip on the pollen grains on the slide and examine under a compound microscope.

In the space below, draw the pollen grains the way they appear under high power magnification.

What do these pollen grains contain that are necessary to fertilize the egg cell?

4. **Lab – "The Food Web Game."** I developed the worksheet below to accompany a very engaging board game that can be purchased from *Carolina Biological Supply Company*. The game is listed in their catalog as "Food Web Game." As discussed in Chapter 6, I tried to include a board game in each of the units as one of the lab activities available for student choice.

# Lab —The Food Web Game

## Introduction

The object of this game is to be the first animal in the food web to collect enough food and use the energy of that food to reach the beginning of the food web – the SUN.

## To Play

To find out how to set up and play the game, read the instructions found inside the game box.

## Questions to Answer After Playing the Game

1. List the members of your group and their places in the game (1st place, 2nd place, etc.)

2. What animal did YOU play?

3. List three things that you ate (your role animal).

    a.

    b.

    c.

4. Describe three encounters that you had with other animals, and how each encounter turned out.

    a.

    b.

    c.

5. Describe one adaptation (trait) that your animal has that helps it to survive.

6. Working with the other people in your group, construct (on one sheet of paper) the food web represented in this game. Be sure to put all of your names on the food web diagram.

5. **Lab – "The Cell Membrane and Osmosis."** I used this lab as one of the choices on the menu in the cell biology unit. This activity helps students to visualize the cellular process of osmosis because the cells that they will use in the lab are macroscopic—they're chicken eggs! I found that the easiest way to prepare the eggs for this lab is to immerse the eggs in white vinegar for forty-eight hours before doing the lab activity. The acid in the vinegar will remove the calcium from the egg shell, leaving a soft rubbery, semipermeable membrane. It's a good idea after this forty-eight-hour period to carefully rinse the eggs and then store them in a large glass container (restaurant institution-size jars work well)

of tap water. Be sure to warn the students to handle the eggs with care! You will also need to prepare the 10 percent and 5 percent salt solutions ahead of time and store them in large glass jars as well. The easiest solution to prepare will be the 0 percent salt solution because it's just deionized water. A helpful note: After the students use the eggs, they can be reused; just have the students place them back into the storage jar containing tap water.

## Lab —The Cell Membrane and Osmosis

### Introduction

Water is the most abundant substance in any cell. All of the chemical processes of the cell involve water in some way. Water passes into and out of the cell by **osmosis**. Osmosis is the diffusion of water molecules through a **semipermeable membrane** from an area where the concentration of water molecules is high to an area where the concentration of water molecules is lower.

The cell membrane is a semipermeable membrane. It allows some substances to pass through while blocking others. Because water molecules are relatively small, they easily pass through the tiny pores in the cell membrane. If the cell is in an environment where the concentration of water molecules is greater outside than inside the cell (**hypotonic** environment), more water will move through the cell membrane into the cell by osmosis than out of it. If the concentration of water molecules is greater inside the cell than it is outside, (**hypertonic** environment) then more water will move out of the cell by osmosis than into it.

The amount of water in the cell changes as the cell's environment changes. If too much water enters the cell by osmosis, the cell may be in danger of bursting (**lysis**). If too much water leaves the cell, the cell will shrink and collapse (**plasmolysis**). In the normal environment of the cell, however, the water concentration does not undergo such radical changes.

In this lab, you will use a "raw" chicken egg with its shell removed as a **model** of the cell to demonstrate the process of osmosis. The egg membrane is semipermeable, because the egg really IS a cell!

**Pre-lab Questions**

1. Go to the lab materials table and carefully take one of the eggs out of the jar of water and gently pat it dry with a paper towel. How is the structure of the egg like the cells you have looked at under the microscope? How is it different?

2. Look at the container labeled 10 percent salt solution. What is a 10 percent salt solution (think about how you would explain that to a younger student)?

3. If you placed this chicken egg cell in a beaker of 10 percent salt solution, what do you predict might happen? Why?

4. If you placed this chicken egg cell in a beaker of 0 percent salt solution, what do you predict might happen? Why?

5. What is osmosis?

**Materials**

1 "raw" chicken egg with its shell removed

1 beaker

1 balance

5 percent salt solution

10 percent salt solution

0 percent salt solution

corn syrup

**Instructions**

1. The egg shells were removed by placing the eggs in dilute acetic acid (vinegar) overnight. Handle the egg with extreme care because it is fragile!

2. Pick out one egg and carefully pat it dry with paper towel.

3. Weigh the egg on a balance and record its starting mass in Data Table 1 under "10 percent salt solution."

4. Submerge the egg in a beaker of 10 percent salt water for ten minutes.

5. After ten minutes, take the egg out, pat it dry, and weigh it again. Record this final mass in Data Table 1 under 10 percent salt solution." *Then record this mass as the "starting mass" under "5 percent salt solution."*

6. Submerge the egg in a beaker of 5 percent salt water for ten minutes.

7. After ten minutes, take the egg out, pat it dry, and weigh it again. Record this final mass in Data Table 1 under 5 percent salt solution." *Then record this mass as the "starting mass" under "0 percent salt solution."*

8. Submerge the egg in a beaker of 0 percent salt water for ten minutes.

9. After ten minutes, take the egg out, pat it dry, and weigh it again. Record this final mass in Data Table 1 under 0 percent salt solution."

10. Calculate the changes in the mass of the egg and record them in Data Table 1.

## Data Table 1

| | 10% salt water | 5% salt water | 0% salt water |
|---|---|---|---|
| Starting Mass | | | |
| Final Mass | | | |
| Change in Mass (+ or -) | | | |

## Post-lab Questions

1. Was there any change in your egg after it sat in the 10 percent salt water for ten minutes? Use your actual data about mass before and after in your explanation. If there were any changes, explain how and why these changes occurred.

2. Was there any change in your egg after it sat in the 5 percent salt water for ten minutes? Use your actual data about mass before and after in your explanation. If there were any changes, explain how and why these changes occurred.

3. Was there any change in your egg after it sat in the 0 percent salt water for ten minutes? Use your actual data about mass before and after in your explanation. If there were any changes, explain how and why these changes occurred.

4. Think about what happened to the egg in this activity. How was the behavior of the egg like the behavior of the cells that make up your own body?

5. Along with osmosis, what are some other ways that cells move materials into or out of themselves? Why are these processes important?

## Lab Follow-up Experiment

1. Take the egg and carefully pat it dry.

2. Place the egg in a beaker of corn syrup.

3. Carefully observe the egg in the corn syrup for ten minutes.

4. In the space below, record your observations of the egg as it sits in the corn syrup.

5. Explain what you think is causing the changes that you are observing.

6. When finished, carefully rinse off all the corn syrup from the egg before placing it back in the jar of eggs on the lab supplies table.

6. **Lab – "Building Models of Molecules."** Here's another lab activity that I used in the cell biology unit. Since my ninth graders had not taken a chemistry course yet, this hands-on, delicious activity helped the students to begin to understand the connection between atoms and some biologically important molecules.

## Lab— Building Models of Molecules

### Introduction - Purpose

Sometimes chemists and biochemists will build three-dimensional models of molecules that they are studying. These models, because they are more realistic than two-dimensional drawings, help them to better understand how the molecules are able to function the way that they do.

**The purpose of this activity is to build three-dimensional models of some biologically important molecules.**

## Materials

gumdrops (several different colors)

toothpicks

glue or glue gun

mounting board

## Instructions

1. Using different colored gumdrops (for example, use black for carbon, white for oxygen, and red for hydrogen) to represent atoms, and toothpicks to represent bonds, build structural models of the following molecules.

| Molecule | Chemical Formula | Structural Formula |
|---|---|---|
| Oxygen gas | $O_2$ | $O = O$ |
| Hydrogen gas | $H_2$ | $H - H$ |
| Methane gas | $CH_4$ | $H - \overset{\overset{\displaystyle H}{\mid}}{\underset{\underset{\displaystyle H}{\mid}}{C}} - H$ |
| Carbon dioxide | $CO_2$ | $O = C = O$ |
| water | $H_2O$ | $H \diagup \overset{O}{} \diagdown H$ |

glucose $C_6H_{12}O_6$ (See your textbook for a diagram.)

the amino acid alanine $C_3H_7O_2N$ (See your textbook for a diagram.)

2. Glue your three-dimensional models to a display board of cardboard or foam core board. Be sure to include a title, labels, and a key explaining what colors were used for the different types of atoms.

7. **Lab – "Cell Structures and Functions Board Game."** I discovered that not only do the students enjoy playing educational board games (with accompanying worksheets to hold them accountable), but board games also provide a great way for the students to learn by doing while they practice the essential 21st century skills of collaboration, communication, and critical thinking. This activity was also one of the choices on the cell biology unit menu. You can find this activity for download at the following site:

**https://www.teacherspayteachers.com/Product/
Cell-Structures-Functions-Board-Game-6615472**

8. **Internet Activity – "Cloning."** There are some excellent interactive websites that provide engaging learning activities for students, and the https://learn.genetics.utah.edu site is one of the absolute best. To produce the following activity sheet, I worked through the Cloning option on this genetics site as a student would, and wrote the activity sheet as I worked through the site. This activity could be used by students in either a cell unit or in a genetics unit. The students enjoyed this activity, especially the part where they virtually cloned a cartoon mouse on the computer screen!

### Internet Activity Cloning

#### Introduction

1. Go to the following website:

**learn.genetics.utah.edu/content/tech/cloning/**

2. Click on the link entitled "What is Cloning?" Answer the questions below as you explore that link.

3. Name two clones that you know **PERSONALLY**.

    a.

    b.

4. Explain how cloning using the process of **artificial embryo twinning** works. Use the following terms in your description: early embryo, Petri dish, and surrogate mother.

5. Explain how cloning using somatic cell nuclear transfer works. Use the following terms in your description: somatic cell from adult sheep, egg cell from adult sheep, somatic cell nucleus, egg cell nucleus, surrogate mother, and Dolly the clone.

6. How is an embryo that is created by **artificial embryo twinning** different from an embryo that is created by **somatic cell nuclear transfer**?

7. Now go back to the cloning homepage and click on the link entitled "Click and Clone." On this page, you will be able to clone a mouse (a virtual lab activity!) on the screen.

8. Work through this cloning activity.

9. What five tools will you need to clone Mimi?

    a.

    b.

    c.

    d.

    e.

10. What mouse donated the egg?

11. What did you use the blunt pipette for?

12. What did you use the sharp pipette for?

13. What did you transfer into the **enucleated** egg?

14. What is the early embryo called when it is a ball of sixteen cells?

15. What was the name of the surrogate mother mouse?

16. Click on the link entitled "The History of Cloning."

17. In what year were the first animals artificially cloned?

18. What animals were they?

19. How did Hans Spemann clone salamanders in 1902?

20. In 1952, Briggs and King cloned a frog by nuclear transfer. Where did they get the donor nucleus?

21. Why are mammals harder to clone than amphibians?

22. Who cloned the first mammal?

23. What large mammal was cloned in 1987?

24. In 1996, what did the two little lambs, Megan and Morag teach us?

25. Compared to all of the cloning experiments up until 1996, what was so special about Dolly?

26. Neti and Ditto were two clones produced in 1997. What kind of animals were they?

27. Now go back to the cloning homepage and click on the link entitled "Is it Cloning? Or Not?" Play the game, and when you get to the screen which shows your final score, either print out that screen and attach it to this lab, or (if you are working in the classroom) call the teacher over to look at your screen and sign off below.

**Score:**_____**Teacher's Signature:** _____

9. **Internet Activity – "Stem Cells."** There are some excellent interactive websites that provide engaging learning activities for students, and the https://learn.genetics.utah.edu site is one of the absolute best. To produce the following activity sheet, I worked

through the Stem Cell option on this genetics site as a student would, and wrote the activity sheet as I worked through the site. This activity could be used by students in either a cell unit or in a genetics unit.

**Internet Activity STEM CELLS**

Stem cells have been a hot topic in biology and medicine in recent years. In this activity, you will learn about where these special cells come from and how they can be used. To get started, go to this site:

**http://learn.genetics.utah.edu/content/tech/stemcells/**

**Click on the activity entitled "The Nature of Stem Cells" and answer the following questions as you work through that activity:**

1. What are differentiated cells?

2. What is an undifferentiated cell?

3. In a human embryo, how long after fertilization does the blasto-cyst stage occur?

4. Draw a blastocyst and label the cells on the outside of the embryo as well as the inner cell mass.

5. What will the outer layer of cells of the blastocyst become?

6. What will the cells of the inner cell mass become?

7. Two weeks after fertilization, the embryo organizes itself into three layers of cells. List two body parts that develop from each of the three types of embryo cells:

ectoderm –

mesoderm –

endoderm –

8. Even after embryo development, when a person is a child, adolescent, or adult, there are still pockets of stem cells scattered throughout the body. What are these special stem cells called?

9. List three places in an adult's body where stem cells can be found.

**Click on the link entitled "Stem Cell Quick Reference" and answer the questions below.**

1. Read the section entitled "Embryonic Stem Cells." How many different kinds of body cells can embryonic stem cells develop into?

2. What ethical considerations come into play when using embryonic stem cells?

3. Read the section entitled "Somatic Stem Cells." What is one disadvantage of using adult stem cells rather than embryonic stem cells?

4. What ethical considerations come into play when using adult stem cells?

5. Read the section entitled "Induced Pluripotent Stem Cells." What kinds of cells can be turned (in the lab) into induced pluripotent stem cells?

6. What can pluripotent stem cells be turned into?

7. What ethical considerations come into play when using induced pluripotent stem cells?

8. Read the section entitled "Therapeutic Cloning." In terms of organ and tissue transplants, what advantage could therapeutic cloning provide?

9. What ethical considerations come into play when using therapeutic cloning?

**Click on the activity entitled "Unlocking Stem Cell Potential."**

1. What is regeneration?

2. Give an example of regeneration.

3. What kinds of cells does regeneration depend on?

4. For the most part, our stem cells just _____

_____, they don't replace _____ _____

_____.

5. In regenerative medicine, what are medical researchers hoping to use adult stem cells for?

6. What are tissue engineers **already** doing?

7. What exciting stem cell research results were seen in laboratory rats with damaged spinal cords?

8. Explain how induced pluripotent stem cells have been used to cure mice of sickle cell anemia.

9. If we learn how _____ _____ growth and development are _____, then we may be able to develop new _____ for treating _____.

10. **Lab – "Human Embryo Development and Pregnancy Board Game."** I discovered that not only do the students enjoy playing educational board games (with accompanying worksheets to hold them accountable), board games provide a great way for the students to learn by doing while they practice the essential 21st century skills of collaboration, communication, and critical thinking. I used this activity as one of the choices on my Genetics Part 1 unit menu, which covered mitosis, meiosis, and chromosome disorders (Genetics Part 2 covered genes and Mendelian genetics). You can find this activity for download at the following site:

**https://www.teacherspayteachers.com/Product/The-Human-Embryo-Development-and-Pregnancy-Board-Game-755815**

11. **Lab – "Creature Feature."** I have had my students do simulations of human karyotyping and many times I have seen them get so bogged down in the tedious minutiae of matching up and gluing forty-six chromosomes to their karyotype charts, that they lose their focus on the point of the lesson—to determine the chromosomal abnormality of their "patient." Creature Feature is a karyotyping lab (modified from an original version by Dr. Jon Hendrix of Ball State University) that involves, not humans with forty-six chromosomes, but mythical creatures with only five to seven pairs of chromosomes. With this activity, they still get to experience matching up homologous pairs of chromosomes and constructing a karyotype, but the focus of the lesson is on analyzing and problem solving.

**If you would like for your students to do this fun activity, go to my website: joeruhlteacherpdspeaker.net and download the documents entitled "Creature Feature Lab," "Creature Feature Metaphase Spreads," and "Creature Feature Lab Answer Key."**

12. **Worksheet – "Genetics: Guest Speaker – Gregor Mendel."** This video and accompanying worksheet can be found here:

**https://www.teacherspayteachers.com/Product/ Genetics-Guest-Speaker-Gregor-Mendel-779513**

This video is a recording of Gregor Mendel's visit to my classroom!

13. **Lab – "A Dihybrid Cross Between Pea Plants."** The concepts of meiosis, segregation of alleles, genetic probabilities, genotypes, and phenotypes are covered in this lab activity. In this lab, each pair of students will role-play a pair of crossing pea plants. By flipping coins, they will produce imaginary offspring and compare the ratios of their actual offspring to those predicted by the Punnett square. You can find this activity here:

**https://www.teacherspayteachers.com/Product/Genetics-A-Lab-Simulation-of-Mendels-Pea-Plant-Crosses-776359**

**Teaching Tip:** I have found that a set of sixteen or so 2' x 2' white boards (dry erase boards) are among the most useful materials to have on hand in the classroom. They're ideal in situations where students in a small group are working together on some kind of a problem or task that requires them to draw or write on the white board with a dry erase marker. Because of its 2' x 2' size, each person in a group of three or four students can see the white board and contribute to whatever assignment you have given them. **These white boards are not too expensive. To obtain mine, I simply went to a local home improvement/lumber store and purchased a 4' x 8' sheet of ¼" thick white melamine board, and had the workers in the store cut it up into 2' x 2' sections.** In Figure 9-1 you can see a group of students using one of the white boards.

**Figure 9-1** Students using a white board

When I wanted my students to practice doing Mendelian genetics problems, we would break out of our usual routine of student-directed, student-choice work, and focus for that day on a whole-class activity. I would divide the class up into groups of three students each. I was careful, before the students arrived, to make up the groups myself so that each group had an academically strong student, a weak student, and an average student. Each group was given a 2' x 2' white board, a white board marker, and an eraser. Then I would give each student a copy of a set of Mendelian Inheritance Practice Problems. I told the students to work through the problems one at a time on the white board, where everyone in the group could see the work. I instructed the students to "think out loud," that is, talk about each problem as they worked it out on the white board. When they finished a problem, they were instructed to copy the work on their paper, erase the white board, and then proceed with the next problem. I told them, "When your group is finished with all of the problems, call me over."

As the groups worked on the problems, much to my delight, I discovered that because the problems required critical thinking, specifically application and analysis level thinking, the individuals within each group depended on each other more, providing a sort of "glue" that insured the group members would work collaboratively rather than individually. While the groups worked, I circulated throughout the classroom. When a group got "stuck" they would call me over and I was then able to sit down with them, "shoulder to shoulder," and teach to the group's specific questions as I wrote on their board. When a group finished the problems, I would give each person in that group a copy of the answer key that showed not only the answers, but how to work on each of the problems step-by-step. As I gave them the answer keys, I told them, "Check each of your answers with the answer key. If you missed any, make sure you figure out why you missed them. If you can't figure out why, then call me over." Happily, this practice turned out to be one of those "works every time" teaching strategies, so here are the practice genetics problems that I used, along with the answer key:

### 14. <u>Worksheet – "Mendelian Inheritance Practice Problems."</u>

**Mendelian Inheritance Practice Problems**

1. Given an individual with the genotype AABb, list all the possible gene combinations that could show up in this person's sex cells.

2. PKU is a recessive condition. If two parents are both heterozygous (carriers) and they have eight children, how many of their children would probably have PKU disease?

3. Cystic fibrosis is recessive. If a normal couple has a child with cystic fibrosis, what are the chances that their next child will have a normal phenotype?

4. Tay Sachs disease is caused by an autosomal recessive gene, t. If Mr. and Mrs. Franks are both carriers of the Tay Sachs gene, what is the probability that their next baby will be born with Tay Sachs disease?

5. In humans, ostrich feet is dominant to normal. Dwarfism is also dominant. From the following mating, what is the probability that their next child will have the same genotype as his parents?

FfDd x FfDd

Tay Sachs disease is caused by an autosomal recessive gene, t. The pedigree chart below illustrates a family with individuals who were born with this condition. Use the chart below to answer the following questions. In this pedigree, shaded-in symbols represent affected individuals. T represents the normal allele and t represents the allele for Tay Sachs disease.

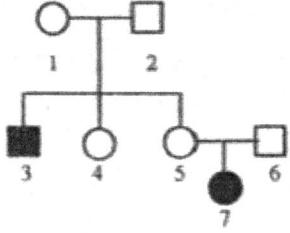

6. What is the genotype of individual #3?

7. What is the phenotype of individual #3?

8. What are the probable genotypes of individuals #1 and #2?

9. How do you know?

10. What is the probability that individual #5 is a carrier?

What is the probability that individual #4 is a carrier?

Sex-linked traits are caused by genes located on one of the sex chromosomes. Specifically, X-linked genes are on the X chromosome. An example of an X-linked trait is hemophilia (bleeder's disease). The pedigree below shows the inheritance of hemophilia in a family. Use the information in the pedigree to answer the following questions. Females who are carriers have the genotype $X^H X^h$. Males who are normal have the genotype $X^H Y$. Males who have hemophilia have the genotype $X^h Y$.

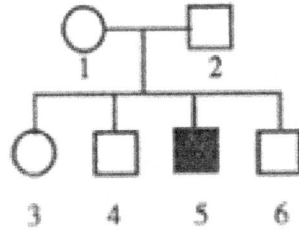

11. What is the genotype of individual #1?

12. What is the genotype of individual #2?

13. What is the genotype of individual #5?

14. Construct a Punnett square to illustrate all the possible genotypes that could show up in the children of individuals #1 and #2.

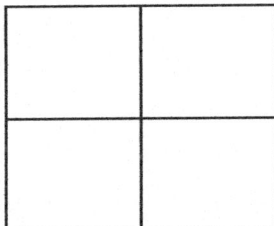

15. Looking at the pedigree chart of this family, according to this Punnett square, what is the probability (if they decide to have another baby) that their fifth child will be a girl with hemophilia?

16. What is the probability (if they decide to have another baby) that their fifth child will be a boy with hemophilia?

**Answer Key for Mendelian Inheritance Practice Problems**

You can download the answer key for the Mendelian Inheritance Practice Problems from my website here:

**joeruhlteacherpdspeaker.net**

**Teaching Tip:** Acting Out Protein Synthesis.

Protein synthesis, involving transcription of mRNA and then translation to produce proteins is a process that is not easy for ninth graders to visualize. Before getting into the molecular details of this cellular process, I found it useful to have students play the parts of the key molecules and act it out. If you check out the video of my Genetics students acting out protein synthesis, you might find some ideas for how you could adapt such a role-playing activity into your own classroom. You will notice that the only materials needed for this activity are paper grocery bags, index cards, papers clips, Scotch tape, a lab coat, and a hard hat. Here's the link to our dramatization of protein synthesis:

**https://youtu.be/daDeK0M2Rg8**

15. **Lab – "Recombinant DNA and Bacterial Transformation Board Game."** Since the information needed for students to play this game (and answer the questions in the accompanying worksheet) can be found on the game board and the playing cards themselves, this game could be used to *introduce* the topics of restriction enzymes, gene splicing, ligase, recombinant DNA, genetic engineering, and bacterial transformation—materials and processes that are basic to modern molecular genetics techniques. The game

could also be used as a *review* at the end of a unit. I have found this game to be a good way to teach students the basics of these molecular biology techniques before having them do an actual bacterial transformation lab.

You can find this activity for download at the following site:

**https://www.teacherspayteachers.com/Product/Recombinant-DNA-and-Bacterial-Transformation-Board-Game-766529**

# CHAPTER 10

# How to Set Up a Science Research Projects Course

For the last twenty-three years of my teaching career, I developed and ran a Science Research Projects course for juniors and seniors, who were interested in science or engineering careers, and it was listed in our school's course catalog along with a host of other honors courses. But it took a fair amount of work on the front end to get the course approved and on the books. Teacher training courses offered in colleges and universities do a pretty job of preparing young teachers regarding teaching philosophies and methods, but I discovered that learning how to deal with the politics and "administrivia" of school culture requires on the job training; another example of how grit and refusal to give up is vital in teaching. In 1997, when I proposed to our administration that I wanted to develop a Science Research Projects course that would allow the students to work in science or engineering labs at nearby Purdue University, I was first met with a bit of institutional inertia. I learned that sometimes we teachers need to be willing to be "salespersons," lobbyists, negotiators, and advocates; roles that are not spelled out in our list of expectations for teachers, but which are necessary in order to get anything done. Getting this course approved required me to first convince my administration that such a course would be valuable, and then to write up a course description and proposal, which went to a school corporation curriculum committee for approval. This was a little tricky because a few teachers, who served on the curriculum committee of course, had concerns about how the addition of a new science course might affect student enrollments in their own subject areas. After a fair amount of discussion and written memos, my proposal was accepted and approved. Then it went to the school board for final approval, where happily, it was finally approved.

I ran this course from 1998 through 2020 when I retired, and we were fortunate to be just a ten-minute drive from Purdue University. This kind of a course is easier to run if your school is near a college or university, where high school students are welcomed to work in their labs. A projects course like this could also be made available to students in schools that are not located near research institutions, but the advantage of being near a college is that the students are able to engage in authentic, cutting-edge research with access to experts in their area, as well as materials and equipment not commonly found in high school science labs. Figure 10-1 shows how the course description appeared in our school's course catalog.

Figure 10-1Science Research Projects Course

## SCIENCE RESEARCH, INDEPENDENT STUDY - HONORS

**Full year course, 1 credit per semester** (may be repeated for more than one year) – *Prerequisites: Current enrollment in Chemistry I or I H or have passed the first semester of Chemistry I or I H. Recommended students should have passed or currently be enrolled in Physics l or Physics l H.* (DOE Course Code: 3008)

This is a laboratory course.

The purpose of this course is to allow students with a strong interest in science to conduct independent scientific research. Students are expected to present the finished product in one or more science fair competitions. A student's acceptance into the course is determined by a screening committee based upon information gathered from the following: a letter of application from the student, consistent achievement test scores in science at or about the 95th percentile or a composite score at or above the 92nd percentile, attendance records, grades, the *Secondary Science Teacher's Referral*, which is filled out by the candidate's former or present science teacher, and an interview with the high school honors science research teacher.

Our school ran on a block schedule, which meant that there were four ninety-two-minute periods per day, so each class met every *other* day for ninety-two minutes, unlike the old "normal" schedule in which each class met every day for fifty-two minutes. Fortunately, our school already had a practice in place of allowing certain juniors and seniors the opportunity for "release time" from the school campus if they had a history of exhibiting responsible behavior, if they were on track to achieve the number of credits required for graduation, or if they were on a school-related vocational work program that allowed them to leave the school grounds early to go to a job off campus. Having this "release time" policy in place certainly helped when I lobbied for allowing the kids in my course to leave at the beginning of fourth hour (around 1:30, the last period of the day) so they could travel to Purdue and work in their labs until their mentors went home for the evening. Most of our juniors and seniors drove to school so they were able to provide their own transportation to the university. Those who didn't drive either rode with a classmate or rode the city bus that conveniently had a stop in front of our school building, and students were able to get free city bus passes for the entire school year. In the spring, near the end of the school year, I found it helpful to "tactfully and diplomatically nag" and remind the administrator in the guidance department who was responsible for building the next year's class schedule that the Science Research Projects course needed to be scheduled for last period of the day.

During the summers of 2009 and 2010, I had the opportunity to work in the molecular genetics lab of the Purdue Department of Forestry and Natural Resources, thanks to Dr. Andrew DeWoody, allowing me to make a little extra money while learning about new molecular genetics lab techniques. In that summer job, my mentors were a couple of graduate students, who were half my age and who, fortunately, were very sweet and patient with me, because I was completely clueless for at least the first few weeks! As it turns out, that humbling experience gave me the understanding and empathy that enabled me to help and encourage my students who always struggled and felt like "deer in headlights" when they first started working in their university labs. Inevitably, these talented, hard-working honors students, with encouragement and just being pointed in the right direction, were able to soar to impressive heights. Near the end of the school year when it was time for the regional science fair, I always loved it when the students would present the results and conclusions of their research as they practiced their presentations. Since I'm a biologist, if a student presented their work in some field of science or engineering other than biology, most of the time their presentations went entirely over my head! That was such a joyful and rewarding thing for me to experience! It reminded me of how gifted and talented honors students can achieve beyond our expectations if we just give them real-world challenges. During that twenty-three-year period, over three hundred students participated in this program and I am forever indebted to the many Purdue researchers who were more than willing to share their expertise, time, and lab space with these budding scientists. In most cases, a student ended up working closely with a graduate student on a small piece of their mentor's overall research area. Many of these students ended up as co-authors with their mentors on papers that were published in refereed scientific journals. As I looked back at the records over that twenty-three-year period, I noticed that about 75 percent of those students were females. The most rewarding part of this program is that many of the students ended up pursuing professional careers and even Ph.D.s in programs related to their high school project work. For a snapshot of my Science Research Projects course, take a look at the article here:

https://engineering.purdue.edu/MSE/news/2020/
early-steps-toward-purdue-research-jefferson-hs

If you are interested in starting up a similar course at your school, check out the following timeline and appendices, so you won't have to "reinvent the wheel!"

**The Timeline and "Nuts and Bolts" of Setting Up and Running a Science Research Projects Course** (*Of course, you will need to adjust the dates that I have referred to in this timeline as well as in the documents in the appendices.*)

1. **Early May** - Get from the office a list of students who will be enrolled in the Science Research course in the upcoming fall semester.

2. **Before summer vacation begins** - Meet with each of the students signed up for the fall, to find out what their research interest area is. Get their phone numbers and email addresses so they can be contacted during the summer.

3. **During the summer** - Find university mentors for each of the students. The easiest way to do this is, for example, if you have a student interested in chemical engineering, email the chemical engineering department head, and ask them to forward your request to anyone in the department who they think might be interested. **See the document entitled "Mentor Request" in Appendix 1 for the main body of said email.** After a week or two, you will get emails from interested researchers. Here's how I find the emails for the department heads:

   a. Google (for example) "Purdue Biology Department." And then go to "faculty directory." There you can see the department head's email/phone number and the emails/phone numbers of the faculty members.

   b. Departments that I have contacted for mentors in the past:

   Biology

   Veterinary Medicine

Biochemistry

Entomology

Botany & Plant Pathology

Agronomy

Animal Science

Horticulture

Chemistry

Engineering (all areas: chemical, nuclear, agricultural, electrical, mechanical, materials, civil, etc.)

Computer Science

Computer Technology

Physics

Psychology

c.  I have found that finding the mentors for each of the students is a fair amount of work in the summer, but when it's completed, you will find that the summer work was worth it. When school starts in August, then the kids can hit the ground running! During the school year, the mentors become the teachers of this course and you will be administering—making sure the kids are meeting deadlines and that their paperwork (rules forms) are in order.

4. **During the summer** - Each time a mentor is secured, contact the student, and tell them to go ahead and set up an initial get-acquainted meeting with that mentor.

5. **First week of school** - Give each student a copy of the Science Research Course grading policy, which includes their deadlines throughout the school year. **See the document entitled "Science Research Course Grading Policy" in Appendix 2.** Each of the deadlines is worth ten points. If a student meets the deadline on the

due date, then they receive ten points for that deadline. If one day late, then nine points are given. If two days late, then eight points are given, etc.

6. **First week of school** - Go to the website: https://www.society-forscience.org/isef/international-rules/, download and print the science fair rules forms that each student and mentor must fill out (one-sided). Since URLs may change from year to year, you can also Google "Intcl ISEF" to find, download, and print the rules forms. They must be printed out (for the students and mentors to fill out) one-sided.

**These rules forms are essential if one of your students is fortunate enough to qualify to advance from your local regional or state science fair to the _International Science and Engineering Fair (ISEF)_.**

7. **Mid-August** - Email a copy of the rules forms to each mentor along with the document entitled "Rules Forms Instructions for Mentor," **(as seen in Appendix 3)** as well as a 'thank you' for working with the student this school year **(as seen in Appendix 4)**.

8. **Mid-August** - Distribute to the students the memo listed as "August 13 Instructions" **(As seen in Appendix 5)**. Attach the document entitled "Rules Forms Instructions for Mentor."

9. **September 9** - Students should return the signed release form to you (this pretty much "forces" them (especially if they're shy) to begin meeting with their mentor. **See the document entitled "Jefferson High School Science Research Course Agreement" in Appendix 6.**

10. **October 1** - This is when the written rescrach proposal is due. It will become part of the student's Science Fair Rules Forms packet.

11. **October 8** - This is when the Science Fair Rules forms are due. Since these forms are partly the responsibility of the mentor, I tend to be somewhat lenient on this deadline.

12. **November 11** - This is when a copy of a sample of initial data of the student's work is due. This is just to make sure that the student is making good progress.

13. **Mid-February** - Since form 1C of the rules forms is to be filled out, signed, and dated by the mentor at the end of the experimentation (it can even be before the end), you may have to hound the students and/or mentors to get these returned to you. These will go on the end of the **paper** science fair rules forms. In mid-February, you will need to scan and digitize each student's rules forms (to turn them into PDFs).

14. **End of February** - Make sure your students are registered for your state's nearest regional science and engineering fair.

15. **About a week before the science fair** - Give out to the students the memo entitled "Science Fair Coming Up!" **(See Appendix 7.)**

## Final Thoughts

The students who participated in the Science Research Projects course learned not only about their own research project, but they also grew in confidence and "came out of their shells." They learned so many important lessons such as:

1. How to navigate and find their way around on a large university campus.

2. How to "rub shoulders" with and work alongside graduate students and professors.

3. How to design experiments.

4. How to collaborate with other researchers and consult with experts when faced with difficult problems.

5. How to use university lab equipment.

6. How to problem-solve.

7. How to communicate effectively both in writing and public speaking.

These students, after graduating from high school and going on to college, would often come back to visit and tell me that the Science Research Projects course really gave them a "leg up" advantage when they finally did go off to college. I was so proud of these kids because many times, at the end of the school year, their professors who mentored them would tell me that my students' work was of the quality of a good master's degree student! That's a real tribute to the work that the English, math, chemistry, and physics teachers at our school did in preparing these students for the Science Research Projects course.

Figure 10-2A few of those three hundred plus Science Research Projects Course students

Over the course of twenty-three years, twelve of these students qualified at regional or state science and engineering fairs to advance to the *International Science & Engineering Fair*—a rare and wonderful accomplishment! I was fortunate to be able to accompany those students to those *International Science & Engineering Fairs*. At this international competition, held each May, up to fifteen hundred students representing about seventy different countries and territories present their projects. Some of those high school students, especially ones in engineering, already have patents pending on their inventions! As I strolled through the exhibit halls looking at the projects and talking with the students, I was overwhelmed by how sophisticated the projects were. These were the best and brightest budding young scientists on the planet. A surprising number of these students spoke English and in my conversations with the students, I was so impressed with their intelligence, their eloquence, the passion they exuded for their work, and their compassion and their zeal for solving problems that plague humanity and our planet. There was the young man who designed and built a revolutionary model of a wheelchair. I remember the student who designed and built a special glove with sensors in it that when worn by someone who knew sign language, would automatically generate the text into a Word document on a computer. There were many students who developed new, ingenious ways to limit carbon emissions by industries and automobiles. There were numerous students working on new and effective cancer treatments and possible cures! Talking with these international students filled me with a profound sense of optimism for the future of our world. When I watched the students interacting at the planned social events and dinners, I was struck by how they all seemed to be into the same clothing styles, mannerisms and music, no matter what part of the world they came from. They all got along so well together, exchanging pins (*the Indiana pin had an image of an Indy 500 race car on it!*) and addresses. I remember imagining and wishing, "If only these students could replace some of our world's existing adult, egocentric, power-hungry leaders, maybe there would truly be peace on Earth . . ."

# CONCLUSION

Thank you for letting me reminisce with you in this book. More important than the reminiscences, if you are an educator, I hope you will find some of the ideas I have shared to be useful. Teaching is a noble profession, and I would encourage you, whether you are a veteran teacher or just starting out in the profession, to be strong and hang in there! I know it's hard work, but nothing of value in life, nothing that lasts, ever comes easy. Because the work can drain you physically and emotionally, be sure to take care of yourself by eating right, exercising, carving out time for play, and getting enough sleep (*I confess that getting enough sleep was the thing I probably was not as intentional about as I should have been.*) Most importantly, be sure to take care of your family—your human relationships of first importance. I'm thankful to my wise and wonderful wife Gail. When our children were young, on those school nights when sleepiness started to overtake me while playing board games or reading bedtime stories, she would whisper, gently reminding me, "Reach back!" They grow up too fast, and so I refused to grade papers or do lesson plans until after they went to bed.

I live in Indiana. I know that everyone has their own preferences, but I love the temperate climate here (not *too* hot and not *too* cold). Each of the changing seasons brings its own kind of wonder and newness; the pastoral beauty of song birds and wildflowers in springtime, the warmth and green luxuriousness of summer, the cool, crisp air and breathtaking fall coloration of autumn, and the quiet, sparkling beauty of winter when the world is magically transformed by a fresh, white blanket of newly fallen snow. I'm not a meteorologist, but I do know that weather describes short-term, daily changes in the atmosphere, whereas climate describes what the average weather is like over a long period of time. Climate, analogous to a person's personality, and weather, like a person's mood on any given day, are two very different things. Job satisfaction is a bit like climate. I found a long-term career in teaching—like climate—to be richly rewarding and satisfying. Admittedly there were days that, like temporary weather, could be difficult, overcast, and stormy, but overall, I loved the work, and it makes me sad whenever I hear a teacher say, "I would never encourage my child to become a teacher." Is it because of the stress related to the work? I would venture to say that stress comes with any job. Serving voluntarily as a church elder, I've caught a glimpse of the stresses that priests, ministers, rabbis, or imams have in shepherding a flock or congregation; stress in the form of ministering to and sharing the burdens of people who are suffering physically, emotionally, spiritually, or psychologically. People who own restaurants have stresses related to knowing how much perishable food to have on hand and how to keep customers and employees happy. People who are self-employed have financial stresses since many small businesses fail. I know farmers who deal with stress related to fluctuating markets, insect pests, plant diseases, and uncontrollable weather in the form of flood or drought. I've heard doctors, nurses, waiters, waitresses, truck drivers, and lawyers discourage their children from following in the parents' professional footsteps. I think the old adage "the grass is always greener on the other side" is true. Maybe there are some jobs that don't involve stress, but I can't think of any!

Do some teachers discourage their children from becoming teachers because of the low pay? Admittedly, I do remember the years when our children were growing up at home; days when I would sit down to pay monthly bills and temptations of leaving the profession would creep into my head. I guess those temporary moments were like days of stormy weather. It's true; teachers won't get rich according to the world's or Wall Street's definition of wealth, but most people fail to consider the long-term (*analogous to climate*) financial benefits in teaching in the form of relatively inexpensive health insurance paid for mostly by the teacher's employer, employer contributed retirement accounts that can surprisingly grow significantly over time, in addition to a pension (*something that most retired people do not have!*) allowing you to retire comfortably. But if you're not into delayed gratification, you don't have to wait until retirement to enjoy this most noble of professions! While I was teaching, I had the security of being an employee, not an employer. I could be as creative as I wanted to be—a true entrepreneur—without the financial stress caused by worrying about whether my business would succeed or fail.

As I'm sure you've gathered from stories told in this book, there are richer rewards to be gained from a career in teaching that far outweigh the financial rewards. I've been fortunate to have experienced some *extrinsic* rewards. As a teacher, I was invited to the White House twice, so I can relate to one of my all-time movie heroes, Forrest Gump! Only I didn't go to the White House as a football all-American, a Medal of Honor recipient, or a ping-pong champion, but as a teacher![1] The first time was in the fall of 1989. I was the Indiana recipient in science of the *Presidential Award for Excellence in Science Teaching*. I was there with forty-nine-plus science teachers from the other states and U.S. territories along with fifty-plus math teachers from each of the states and U.S. territories. I'll never forget that beautiful fall day, standing in the Rose Garden when President George H.W. Bush stepped forward, reached out his hand, and with a warm smile greeted me with "Welcome to the White House!" I said something like "It's a pleasure to meet you, sir." He was such a gracious, down-to-earth gentleman and he responded with "Well, it's a pleasure to meet *you!*" Visiting with President Bush and First Lady Barbara Bush felt like visiting with warm, friendly next-door neighbors whom we had known for years.

Meeting President George H.W. Bush – October 1989

My wife, Gail, chatting with First Lady Barbara Bush

My second trip to the White House took place in the spring of 2017. This time, I was with four other teachers: Ashli Skura Dreher, a special education teacher and former New York State Teacher of the Year, Jonathan Gillentine, who was a preschool teacher from Hawaii, Matinga Ragatz, who was a social studies teacher and former Michigan State Teacher of the Year, and Bob Williams, a math teacher and former Alaska State Teacher of the Year. The five of us were the 2017 inductees into the *National Teachers Hall of Fame* and we found ourselves escorted into the Oval Office by the security staff. We were hurried in one by one for a quick photograph beside the Resolute Desk, where Donald Trump was sitting. I actually touched the Resolute Desk when I leaned down to shake the hand of the president as he sat there!

It's interesting. The best part of being inducted into the *National Teachers Hall of Fame* wasn't that trip to the Oval Office, but the surprise assembly program a month earlier in the school gymnasium when the honor was announced. It was a Friday morning—April 7, 2017. Because of the relatively large size of our school, assembly programs were normally held in the theater, with half of the student body attending the program for an hour, followed by a repeat performance for the second half of the student body. The only times the entire student body was assembled in the gym were for Friday afternoon pep sessions (just before school dismissal at the end of the day) prior to big games such as football homecoming or the basketball sectional tournament. Our principal, Mark Preston, came over the intercom and announced that we were all to head to the gym for a special assembly program after the school band was released. There was quite a buzz of excitement and confusion in the halls as we all headed down to the gym on that Friday morning; *"Why are we going to the gym?"* *"What's going on?"* *"This is weird!"* *"Did somebody die?"* *"We never have assembly programs in the gym!"* Three of my science department colleagues and I had been instructed beforehand to head down to the floor and position ourselves near the wall behind a microphone and podium that had been set up at one end of the basketball court. I was told that the purpose of this assembly program was to honor the school's *Academic Competition Team* and that we four science teachers would compete against the team in a competition styled after the television game show, *Jeopardy*. I found out later that these three colleagues of mine were in on the ruse! As twenty-two hundred students and their teachers filed into the gym, I glanced down to the bleachers on the opposite end of the basketball court and saw that the school band was assembled as if it were a pep session. The unusual thing I noticed was that there were a couple rows of chairs on the floor alongside our end of the court reserved for VIPs. Some of these VIPs were already seated; members of the Press, the school superintendent Les Huddle, our State Representative Sheila Klinker, member of the Indiana State Senate Ron Alting, the Lafayette mayor Tony Roswarski, and Lindy Whetzel, who I learned later was vice-chair of the board of trustees of the *National Teachers Hall of Fame*. Little did I know, that my wife, my parents, my children, and my grandchildren were huddled backstage with the school secretary and that they were in on this secret as well! When principal Mark Preston stepped up to the microphone, a hush came over the crowd. Mr. Preston is a charismatic, gifted leader, respected and admired by students and staff alike. As of this writing, he's still working there as the principal, and I will always be grateful to him for the way that he has supported the teachers, his love for the kids, and the way that he established a culture of respect, school pride, and *family* in our student body. He announced that we had a special visitor with us from the *National Teachers Hall of Fame* and invited Lindy Whetzel to come to the microphone. That's when my knees suddenly felt weak and my pulse quickened because I knew I had been nominated and that I was "in the running," but I also knew it was such a long shot. Kevin Igo, our department head and chemistry teacher, placed his hand on my shoulder and smiled. When Lindy made the announcement, twenty-two hundred high school students and their teachers erupted in cheers and applause. To say I was overwhelmed would be an understatement! If you'll bear with me, there are several memories from that day that I know I will cherish for the rest of my life. Mr. Preston went back to the microphone and invited "some special visitors to come out from behind the stage." When my entire family walked out and took the remaining seats in the VIP section, I nearly "lost it." Throughout the program, as State Senator Ron Alting, State Representative Sheila Klinker, and Mayor Tony Roswarski made their presentations, I glanced up at the students assembled in the bleachers. You could have heard a pin drop throughout the entire program. I couldn't believe the smiles and the respectful outpouring of love, support and pride exhibited by the kids, most of whom I didn't even know, because we are such a big school. So many kids and teachers throughout the rest of the school day came up and congratulated me with handshakes and hugs, and the pride they exhibited warmed my heart more than anything. I could tell that the kids were proud because this was a teacher from *their* school! They were excited because Jefferson High School has a hurtful, unfair, inaccurate reputation in the greater Lafayette area of being "that big, scary, inner-city school with the lowest standardized test scores" (*In our school, over half the students are labeled as minority students and two-thirds of the students are classified as economically disadvantaged. We even have some students who are homeless.*) Anyone willing to visit our school is shocked to discover a school with gifted teachers, who skillfully and effectively manage to meet the needs of all kinds of kids regardless of their socioeconomic status, interests, or levels of academic ability. They discover a school that represents the strength and beauty seen in the diversity of human beings that make up our country. I'll never forget those respectful young ladies and gentlemen sitting in the stands that day. My feelings that day were a strange paradoxical mix of pride and humility. I was proud because I knew that only five pre-school through twelfth grade teachers from across the country are inducted each year. I was proud of the fact that, up until 2017, I was only the 6th Indiana teacher ever inducted since the first teachers were inducted in 1992. But more than anything, I was humbled by the experience. I realize that such an honor is a *representative* award and not a *best teacher* award. There I stood with three outstanding colleagues who, among many others I know, I believe are just as deserving. There's no such thing as a self-made teacher, and my colleagues and I have learned so much from one another. I've always loved and believed Ken Blanchard's quote "*None of us is as smart as all of us.*" The photograph below was taken during that assembly program. On my right in the photograph is Kevin Igo, our department head and chemistry teacher. Since it's been four decades since I took college chemistry, on numerous occasions, he has helped me with remembering how to prepare chemical solutions needed for some of our biology labs. To my immediate left is astronomy and earth science teacher, Bill Huston. Over the years, I've learned so much from him as he is a master at skillfully combining both fun and humor with academic rigor. To my far left is Debbie Beck, an outstanding physics teacher, with challenging, rigorous academic expectations. Her students rise up and meet her expectations, achieving at the highest levels because of her love for kids and her pedagogical skills. The pride and love that they and all the teachers and administrators in my school demonstrated to me that day is a memory I will always cherish. Remember *the key*? It's *relationships* that matter.

Three of my science department colleagues (from left to right in the photo)—Kevin Igo, Bill Huston, and Debbie Beck were in on the secret.

© John Terhune – USA TODAY NETWORK

It's the relationships that last. Since we still live in the same town that I taught in for the last thirty-six years of my career, I find myself running into former students all the time. What a rewarding joy it is to hear their expressions of appreciation when they say how much they loved my class, or how much they were inspired by my class to pursue their careers. Oftentimes I won't recognize them at first, especially the boys who are now grown, balding men with facial hair! One of those encounters still makes me laugh, and it happened in the produce section of the grocery store. I was pushing my shopping cart along when I heard a loud voice: "Mr. Ruhl!" Even before I turned around to acknowledge the person, I said to myself, "Now that's that girl with no filter!" (*You know the type?*) I turned around and sure enough, there she was. She yelled (*People were now looking!*), "You're still alive?!" I think I responded with something like, "Uh, let me check my pulse." I don't know if that kind of encounter would classify as the rewarding type, but it does make me laugh, and laughter is healthy!

So why, with all the challenges, long work hours, special interest groups from outside of education pushing their agendas onto schools, and the lack of financial support and respect from some influential state and national level politicians, have I enjoyed teaching so much? I think it must be because of something I've already referred to in this book: that our brains are wired for loving, giving, cultivating human relationships, and being creative. That's how we're made. I believe that when we choose a profession that allows us to do what our brains are wired for, our job satisfaction is enhanced. Maybe that's why so many teachers, who have hung in there for a long career, feel a rewarding sense of accomplishment, well-being, and fulfillment; that they have made a difference in the world. And it's not only teachers who have attested to this human phenomenon. Check out some quotes from others who have discovered this counterintuitive secret to fulfillment.

In the end, it's not about what you have or even what you've accomplished. It's about who you've lifted up, who you've made better. It's about what you've given back. — **Denzel Washington**

No one has ever become poor by giving. — **Anne Frank**

We make a living by what we get, but we make a life by what we give. — **Winston Churchill**

The unselfish effort to bring cheer to others will be the beginning of a happier life for ourselves. — **Helen Keller**

Only a life lived for others is a life worthwhile. — **Albert Einstein**

A fundamental concern for others in our individual and community lives would go a long way in making the world the better place we so passionately dreamt of. — **Nelson Mandela**

Peace begins with a smile. Smile five times a day at someone you really don't want to smile at. Do it for peace. — **Mother Teresa**

Too old to plant trees for my own gratification, I shall do it for my posterity.—**Thomas Jefferson**

I have an irrepressible desire to live till I can be assured that the world is a little better for my having lived in it. — **Abraham Lincoln**

The purpose of life is to contribute in some way to making things better. — **Robert F. Kennedy**

Focusing your life solely on making a buck shows a certain poverty of ambition. — **Barack Obama**

A life is not important except in the impact it has on other lives. — **Jackie Robinson**

It is more blessed to give than to receive. — **Jesus**

If you want happiness for an hour, take a nap.

If you want happiness for a day, go fishing.

If you want happiness for a month, get married.

If you want happiness for a year, inherit a fortune.

If you want happiness for a lifetime, help someone else. — **Ancient Chinese proverb.**

And finally, a "quote" in the form of a gesture from someone unable to speak. She's a little girl I know who is severely mentally challenged. I remember how she didn't even learn to walk until she was seven years old. She gets the most pleasure out of giving gifts to people. I'll never forget the day she walked up to me and when she slowly opened her clenched little fist, out dropped a wadded-up paper candy wrapper into my outstretched hand. Her mother sensed my look of confusion and said that her daughter was giving me a gift. When I said "thank you," the biggest smile beamed across that little girl's face! Something profound happens in the brain when we give. Even in the brain of a severely mentally challenged child.

Any profession that allows one to love, give, cultivate human relationships, or be creative is going to result in increased job satisfaction. Teaching is not for everyone. It's hard work, but it's worth it. If you feel drawn to a career in teaching, go for it! I know you will be blessed!

## Appendix 1 — Mentor Request

Dear Dr. _____,

My name is Joe Ruhl and for the last 20 years I have taught a Science Research course at Jefferson High School. This two-semester course is designed to allow students with strong interests and aptitudes in science to conduct independent scientific research in areas of personal interest. The students who are enrolled in the course for this fall were screened and selected based upon criteria such as grades, standardized test scores, attendance records, teacher recommendations, and potential career interests.

Throughout the school year, each student in this independent projects course is required to conduct a scientific research project, and then present the results of their work at the *Lafayette Regional Science and Engineering Fair* in early March of 20___.

**Typically, as part of this research course, a Purdue researcher will take a student "under his/her wing" as a helper—another set of hands—in the field or lab. With our block schedule, the students in this course even have release time to travel to and work at Purdue. In exchange, the mentor "shows the student the ropes," that is, introduces the student to the world of research. My hope is that the mentor and student would then work together to develop a research project that the student could do under the supervision of that Purdue faculty member. Many times the high school student actually works most closely with a graduate student in the mentor's lab.**

We have had several students involved in this type of work in the past. The opportunities for these capable students to work in the real world and to learn from real scientists have been wonderful. In most cases, a student has ended up working on and contributing to one small component of his/her mentor's area of investigation. This has helped the researcher in a small way and helped the student in a big way. Several of our former students have described their research experiences as "the highlight of their high school studies." Many of these students have decided to pursue science research careers as a direct result of their Purdue experiences. I am extremely proud of these students and grateful to Purdue for allowing these kids exciting educational experiences.

The kids in this course are outstanding students—great kids! I always remind them that in return for being allowed to work as a research apprentice in this way, they must always be willing to help out in the lab in any way that they might be needed. (That's the only compensation I can offer the Purdue researcher in return!)

One of my students, Lauren _____, is enrolled in this course and she is interested in any work related to animal behavior or evolution. A couple years ago, she was an outstanding student in my Honors Biology class and she is very hard working, cooperative, polite, intelligent, and insightful. I also remember being especially impressed with her attention to detail.

Would you be willing to forward this information to any researchers in your department who you think might be interested in taking on this student?

Please let me know of your thoughts.

Thanks!

**Joe Ruhl -**

Science Research Course Teacher

Jefferson High School

1801 S. 18th. St.

Lafayette, IN 47905

463-7012 (home)

772-4700 (work)

jruhl21055@aol.com (home)

jruhl@lsc.k12.in.us (work)

## SCIENCE RESEARCH COURSE
## 2019-20

J. Ruhl

5/19

The purpose of this course is to allow students with a strong interest in science to conduct independent scientific research in an area of personal interest. Students will be expected to enter their projects in the *Lafayette Regional Science and Engineering Fair*

**March 13, 2020.**

**Grading Policy**

Throughout each nine-week grading period, several major components of the course project will be due. The deadlines **(weekly meetings with Mr. Ruhl and project component deadlines)** are listed below. The grade in the course is based upon the successful completion of each of these deadlines.

Each project component deadline will be worth 10 points. (See pages 2 and 3 of this packet.) For each assignment, one point will be deducted for each day late. For each nine-week-period, if a student satisfactorily meets each of the deadlines, he/she will receive an A for the nine-weeks (elevated to A+ as this is an honors science class).

**Weekly Meetings with Mr. Ruhl -**

**Not all Science Research students are scheduled in the same period, so it is rare that the teacher is able to communicate with *all* of the students simultaneously. Therefore, each student will be required to drop in and meet at least once a week with Mr. Ruhl (room 2A1B) to provide an update on the progress made upto that time. These meetings are brief and can be done any time before Friday, 3:30 p.m. of each week. Each weekly meeting is worth five points. If you show up any time during**

the week for this meeting, you will receive five points. If you don't meet at all, then you will receive zero points for that particular week.

## Project Component Deadlines -

| Date | Deadline |
| --- | --- |

**(first nine-week-period):**

| Date | Deadline |
| --- | --- |
| Sept. 3 | selection of mentor and establishment of research site work schedule |
| Sept. 9 | completed and signed release form (includes parent and principal signatures—allowing for release to research site) |
| Oct. 1 | written research proposal (project idea), which includes: |

    a. the statement of the problem to be investigated

    b. hypothesis

    c. an outline of a general plan of investigation, which includes materials and a preliminary procedure

    d. bibliography with *five references*

| | |
| --- | --- |
| Oct. 8 | ISEF rules forms |

## (second nine-week-period):

Nov. 11        a copy of a sample of initial quantitative data generated by the experiment(s)

## (third nine-week-period):

Jan. 6        experimental data (I want copies of your tables, charts, observations in raw data form—not paragraphs.)

Feb. 3        data analysis (This must be one-page—typed—telling what happened in your experiment. Explain your data.)

Feb. 7        a copy of your abstract

Feb. 10        Your mentor must approve your display board and final paper, and sign "Release to Participate in Regional Fair" form. This form must be delivered to Mr. Ruhl by this date.

Mar. 2        a.   science fair display (delivered to room 2A1B)

                     b.   a copy of the final paper (Give the teacher one copy and keep one copy for display at the science fair.)

Mar. 13 & 14        Lafayette Regional Science & Engineering Fair at Purdue

## (fourth nine-week-period):

May 4        a.   return of all equipment and thank-you letters to all who assisted

                     b.   submission of topic area for the following year (if continuing on)

                     c.   continued work in mentor's lab until the end of spring semester

## Attendance Policy

You may or may not have a specific period of the day when you are scheduled for this course (The State Department of Education has waived the "seat time requirement." In other words, you might not have had room in your schedule for this course, but your guidance counselor was able to tack on this course as an extra—possibly a "zero" hour.) That's okay, because scientific research cannot and does not take place only one period every other day. Historically, in this course, students have worked many hours beyond the regularly scheduled time block. Indeed, it is essential in this course to put in the time outside of regular school hours. This is not a traditional class with homework, quizzes, and tests, although the "homework" you do on your own will be extensive. There is a great deal of flexibility built into the program. If you ARE scheduled in this course during a particular period, you will not be allowed to leave the school to work with your mentor until you have turned in to the teacher the signed Science Research Course Release Form. If you must leave school before this form is completed and turned in, you must have a parent call in, giving the school permission for school release during class. Whenever you do leave to work on research (even after the release form has been turned in) you must notify the Science Research course teacher sometime during the day before class begins, so that you will not be counted absent.

If you are scheduled for the Science Research course any period during the regular school day, you will have the following options (listed in order of preference):

    a.   leave the school campus to work with the Purdue mentor

    b.   read any research articles assigned by the mentor

    c.   work on any aspect of the research project

    d.   do homework or study for any other class

Congratulations on being accepted into the Science Research course. You have already proven yourself in terms of your academic ability, your work ethic, and your strong sense of responsibility. Jefferson High School students have earned the *Outstanding School Award* at the *Lafayette Regional Science Fair* in fourteen out of the last nineteen years. As a member of this class, you will have the opportunity to continue a strong tradition of science fair excellence at Jefferson High School. More importantly, you will have a unique opportunity that few high schools can offer. Based upon my conversations with former Science Research course students, I know you will find yourself at a distinct advantage when you go to college—no matter what you major in—but especially if you choose a science-related career. I wish for you the very best in the upcoming school year!

If you have any questions about this course, please contact me:

Joe Ruhl

4422 Lake Villa Dr.

W. Lafayette, IN 47906

765-463-7012 (home)

765-772-4700, ext. 2651 (school)

jruhl@lsc.k12.in.us (school)

## Appendix 3 — Rules Forms Instructions for Mentor

### Instructions for Filling out the Science Fair Rules Forms

The rules forms need to be printed out (one side of the paper only, NOT back-to-back) and filled out.

1. **Checklist for Adult Sponsor (1)**

In these forms, I (Mr. Ruhl) will sign where it says "Adult Sponsor". You (the university mentor) will sign in the places labeled "Supervising Adult," "Designated Supervisor," or "Qualified Scientist."

This first form (Checklist for Adult Sponsor) is not one that you need to worry about. I will fill this one out.

2. **Student Checklist (1A)**

The student will fill out part 1.

Leave part 2 (title) blank for now.

Leave part 7 blank for now.

Once the student gets his/her feet on the ground, he/she can begin working on part 10—a research plan in which he/she describes the tentative project goals.

3. **Research Plan/Project Summary Instructions**

Notice in the instructions on this sheet that the student must include a bibliography (include at least five references).

4. **Approval Form (1B)**

The only thing the student needs to do on this form is for him/her and a parent/guardian to sign in box number 1.

The dates next to the signatures must be **BEFORE** the start date, so the parent/guardian must put down the date when they first gave permission to work on this project. It can be an estimate.

5. **Regulated Research Institutional/Industrial Setting Form (1C)**

This form must be filled out by you, the mentor, at the end of the research experience (or CLOSE to the end)—late February 2020.

6. **Qualified Scientist Form (2)**

This form is to be filled out by you, the mentor, before experimentation begins.

7. **Risk Assessment Form (3)**

This form is to be filled out by you, the mentor, before experimentation begins.

8. **Vertebrate Animal Form (5B)** – only if working with vertebrates

This form is to be filled out by you, the mentor, before experimentation begins.

9. **Potentially Hazardous Biological Agents Risk Assessment Form (6A)**

This form is to be filled out by you, the mentor, before experimentation begins.

10. **Human and Vertebrate Animal Tissue Form (6B)**

This form is to be filled out by you, the mentor, before experimentation begins.

11. **Continuation/Research Progression Projects Form (7)**

This form is to be filled out by the student (with your help) IF the student is continuing a project that he/she started in your lab last year.

## Appendix 4 — Thank You to Mentor

Dear Dr. (name),

Thank you so much for your willingness to mentor (name), by allowing (him/her) to work in your lab this school year. As you know, (name's) work with you is an integral part of our Science Research course that he is enrolled in. The grades that the students in the course earn are based upon the timely completion of deadlines throughout the school year. (I, of course, will keep track of all of those deadlines and assign the grades.) I have attached the policies and deadlines for the course for your information.

Since "kids will be kids," even the good ones, please let me know if (name) is ever late or fails to show up for a meeting or an appointment.

Again, in view of your busy schedule, I sincerely appreciate the time and efforts put in by you and your graduate student(s) in helping this high school research apprentice. Please remember that in exchange for being mentored, (name) is expected to help out in any way that he might be needed.

Thanks!
Joe Ruhl
Science Research Course Teacher
Jefferson High School
Lafayette, IN
765-772-4700 ext. 2651
jruhl@lsc.k12.in.us

## Appendix 5 —August 13 Instructions

August 13, 2019

TO: Science Research Students

FROM: Mr. Ruhl

RE:Science Fair Rules Forms

Well, we're "back in the saddle!" Hope you had a nice summer vacation!

I have attached to this memo a copy of the Science Fair Rules Forms, along with instructions for your mentor on how to fill them out. The instructions are written TO the mentor, but they will help you also in knowing how to fill out the forms. **I will be emailing these rules forms and instructions to your mentor, along with a 'thank you' for mentoring you this school year.**

Good luck as you start your project work! ☺

# Appendix 6 — Jefferson High School Science Research Course Agreement

**JEFFERSON HIGH SCHOOL SCIENCE RESEARCH COURSE AGREEMENT**

_____
Date

To whom it may concern:

    I (we) _____, being the parent(s) or guardian(s) of _____, do hereby grant permission for our son or daughter to leave the Jefferson High School campus at designated times of the week (agreed upon by the science teacher, the research supervisor/mentor, the school administration, and us) to work in the laboratory of Dr. _____ on his/her research project. I (we) understand that my (our) son or daughter will be responsible for his or her transportation.

_____
Principal

_____
Guidance Counselor

_____
Science Teacher

_____
Research Supervisor/Mentor

_____
Parent/Guardian

## Appendix 7 — Science Fair Coming Up!

March 9, 2020

TO: Honors Biology Students and Science Research Students

FROM: Mr. Ruhl

RE: Purdue Science Fair

Greetings!

I know you have been working extremely hard and now you will have the opportunity to *finally* enjoy the fruits of your labor as you present your work at the Purdue Science Fair Friday night, March 13th!

Some helpful information:

1. Come to Mr. Ruhl's classroom (2A1B) to pick up your poster before 4 p.m. Friday afternoon.

2. The science fair will be on the Purdue Campus in a building called Stewart Center (128 Memorial Mall, West Lafayette, IN 47907). There will be signs directing you when you enter the building.

3. Set your project up in Stewart Center anytime between 3:30 and 5:45 p.m.

4. Your poster must be able to stand up on its own on the table that you will be assigned.

5. Place a printed copy of your final paper on the table in front of your poster along with any lab notebooks containing raw data.

6. Most people eat dinner next door in the Purdue Memorial Union Building after they set up their project. Be sure to be back at your poster by 5:45 p.m.

**Be sure to get a good night's sleep Thursday night.**

**Remember to dress professionally for the judging that will take place from 6:00– 9:30 Friday night. Keep a bottle of water with you during the judging.**

Wear comfortable shoes for long periods of standing by your project!

Maintain eye contact while talking to the judges. Smile!

Be enthusiastic as you talk about your project.

Be confident (yet maintain a spirit of humility) because you are the expert on your project.

Have fun! A few butterflies are normal and actually a good thing because they will get your adrenaline going and make your mind sharp and alert. You've worked hard and now it's time to enjoy.

On the next page is a list of questions that judges often ask. If at all possible, please be present at the awards ceremony on Saturday, March 14th from 2:30–4:30 p.m.

Good luck! ☺

# NOTES

**Introduction**

    1. 2 Tm. 4:7 NIV

**Chapter 1: "42 Years in the Classroom? Are You Crazy?"**

    1. Robert T. Hohler, *I Touch the Future: The Story of Christa McAuliffe,* (New York: Random House, 1986), 155

    2. Charlie Drewes, "II. Pour-Person Plankton Net." https://www.eeob.iastate.edu/faculty/DrewesC/htdocs/toolbox-II.htm

**Chapter 2: The Power of Love in Teaching**

    1. Ken Blanchard and Sheldon Bowles, High Five! None of Us Is as Smart as All of Us, (New York: William Morrow & Company, 2001)

    2. Maxwell King, *The Good Neighbor: The Life and Work of Fred Rogers,* (New York: Abrams Press, 2018)

    3. C.S. Lewis, *The Four Loves,* (London: Geoffrey Bles, 1960)

    4. Matt. 22:39 NIV

**Chapter 3: How Can We Show Our Students That We Care?**

    1. David McCullough, "American History and Americas's Future," Lecture. Hillsdale College  National Leadership Seminar, Phoenix, AZ. February 15, 2005. Print.

    2. Dave Burgess, *Teach Like a Pirate.* (San Diego, CA: Dave Burgess Consulting, Inc., 2012), 69

3. Catarina Rodrigues, "The Learning Pyramid: A Study Plan Game Changer," AIESEC, June, 2021, https://aiesec.at/2021/06/10/the-learning-pyramid-a-study-plan-game-changer/

4. Loren Eisley, *The Unexpected Universe.* (Orlando, FL: Harcourt Brace & Company, 1969), 67

Chapter 4: **Life Lessons I've Learned as a Teacher**

1. *Rocky*, directed by John G. Avildsen (1976; United Artists, 2005), DVD

2. Steve Patterson, "Children: From Stepping on Toes to Stepping on Heart," Courageous Christian Father, June 17, 2017, https://www.courageouschristianfather.com/children-stepping-toes-stepping-heart/#axzz7aIDFUwse

3. Lennart Nilsson, "Lennart Nilsson," Science Photo Library, https://www.sciencephoto.com/collection/lennart-nilsson-

4. *A Christmas Story,* directed by Bob Clark (1983; Metro-Goldwyn-Mayer, 1999), 00:15:05, DVD

5. *Hoosiers*, directed by David Anspaugh (1986; Orion Pictures, 1997), 00:03:46, DVD

6. *Hoosiers*, directed by David Anspaugh (1986; Orion Pictures, 1997), 00:28:31, DVD

Chapter 5: **Risky Behavior**

1. Dave Burgess, *Teach Like a Pirate.* (San Diego, CA: Dave Burgess Consulting, Inc., 2012), 55

Chapter 6: **How Transitioning from a Teacher-centered to a Student-centered Classroom Reignited My Passion for Teaching and My Students' Love for Learning**

1. Dr. Seuss, *How the Grinch Stole Christmas.* (New York: Random House, 1957), 46

2. National Education Association (2010). Preparing 21st Century Students for a Global Society: An Educator's Guide to the "Four Cs." https://dl.icdst.org/pdfs/files3/0d3e72e9b873e0ef2ed780b-f53a347b4.pdf

3. 1 Cor. 13:13 NIV

## Chapter 7: **"May We Live in Interesting Times."**

1. "Evolution," PBS.org, https://www.pbs.org/wgbh/evolution/

2. John H. Walton, *The Lost World of Genesis One.* (Downers Grove, IL: InterVarsity Press, 2009), 7

3. John H. Walton, "Understanding Genesis with John Walton," BioLogos, January 16, 2010, https://biologos.org/resources/understanding-genesis-with-john-walton

4. Judge John E. Jones, "Decision in Kitzmiller v. Dover," Case 4:04-cv-02688-JEJ Document 342, December 20, 2005, https://ncse.ngo/files/pub/legal/kitzmiller/highlights/2005-12-20_Kitzmiller_decision.pdf

5. Kenneth R. Miller, *Finding Darwin's God: A Scientist's Search for Common Ground Between God and Evolution.* (New York: HarperCollins Publishers Inc., 1999)

6. Eugenie Scott, "The Creation/Evolution Continuum," National Center for Science Education, January 22, 2016, https://ncse.ngo/creationevolution-continuum

7. Neil Shubin, *Your Inner Fish: A Journey into the 3.5-Billion-Year History of the Human Body.* (New York: Vintage Books, a division of Random House, Inc., 2008)

8. Richard Dawkins, *The God Delusion.* (New York: Houghton Mifflin Company, 2006); Jerry A. Coyne, *Faith Versus Fact.* (New York: Viking Penguin, an imprint of Penguin Publishing Group, a division of Penguin Random House LLC, 2015)

9. Answers in Genesis, https://answersingenesis.org.

10. Francis Collins, *The Language of God.* (New York: Simon & Schuster, Inc., 2006)---. *The Language of Science and Faith.* (Downers Grove, IL: InterVarsity Press, 2011)

11. Charles Kingsley, "Westminster Sermons," Westminster Sermons, by Charles Kingsley, May 10, 2006, https://www.gutenberg.org/files/18369/18369-h/18369-h.htm

12. Janet Kellogg Ray, *Baby Dinosaurs on the Ark? The Bible and Modern Science and the Trouble of Making it All Fit.* (Grand Rapids, MI: Wm. B. Eerdmans Publishing Co., 2021)

Chapter 8: **Evolution Teaching Resources**

1. Ps. 139:13 NIV

**Conclusion**

1. *Forrest Gump*, directed by Robert Zemeckis (1994; Paramount Pictures Corporation, 2001), 01:24:00, DVD